AROUND THE TEXTS OF
WRITING CENTER WORK

AROUND THE TEXTS OF WRITING CENTER WORK

An Inquiry-Based Approach to Tutor Education

R. MARK HALL

UTAH STATE UNIVERSITY PRESS
Logan

© 2017 by the University Press of Colorado

Published by Utah State University Press
An imprint of University Press of Colorado
5589 Arapahoe Avenue, Suite 206C
Boulder, Colorado 80303

   The University Press of Colorado is a proud member of
         The Association of American University Presses.

The University Press of Colorado is a cooperative publishing enterprise supported, in part, by Adams State University, Colorado State University, Fort Lewis College, Metropolitan State University of Denver, Regis University, University of Colorado, University of Northern Colorado, Utah State University, and Western State Colorado University.

The paper used in this publication meets the minimum requirements of the American National Standard for Information Sciences—Permanence of Paper for Printed Library Materials. ANSI Z39.48-1992

ISBN: 978-1-60732-581-9 (paperback)
ISBN: 978-1-60732-582-6 (ebook)

Library of Congress Cataloging-in-Publication Data

Names: Hall, R. Mark, author.
Title: Around the texts of writing center work : an inquiry-based approach to tutor education / R. Mark Hall.
Description: Logan : Utah State University Press, [2017] | Includes bibliographical references and index.
Identifiers: LCCN 2016034819| ISBN 9781607325819 (pbk.) | ISBN 9781607325826 (ebook)
Subjects: LCSH: Writing centers—Research—Methodology. | Writing centers—Administration. | Tutors and tutoring—Vocational guidance. | English teachers—Vocational guidance.
Classification: LCC PE1404 .H337 2017 | DDC 808/.042071—dc23
LC record available at https://lccn.loc.gov/2016034819

Cover illustration © Excellent backgrounds/Shutterstock

for Thia Wolf
All I really need to know about writing center work I learned from you.

CONTENTS

FIGURES

TABLES

ACKNOWLEDGMENTS

As anyone who has worked in a writing center knows, writing center work is less about writing and more about relationships—building and nurturing them. These relationships sustain and enrich my thinking, indeed, my life. I am enormously grateful to the many people who have generously cultivated relationships with me as I have worked on this book, offering ideas, feedback, support, and encouragement.

First, thanks to the many smart and capable students, staff, faculty, and administrators I have come to know in the six writing centers I've had the good fortune to work in since 1987.

Thanks to Utah State University Press editor, Michael Spooner, and to Laura Furney and her editorial team at University Press of Colorado. Thanks to the anonymous reviewers, whose feedback and questions at once both affirmed the value of my ideas and pushed me to develop them further.

This book has been percolating for a long time, since I taught my first tutor-education course in 2002. Since then, lots of students, colleagues, and friends have contributed much. Special thanks to some of those who will find their influence throughout the pages of this book, which, for me, is a tour of the some of my most valued professional relationships: Reese Carleton, Brian Huot, Mary Rosner, Judith Rodby, Chris Fosen, Kim Jaxon, Sarah Pape, Thia Wolf, Jill Swiencicki, David Martins, Ashlyn Walden, Tony Scott, Lil Brannon, Brad Hughes, Rebecca Nowacek, David Stock, Michele Eodice, Kevin Roozen, Stephanie Vie, Elisabeth Gilbert-Olson, Matt McBride, Megan Lambert, Mary Tripp, Mariana Chao, and Elizabeth Wardle.

Always a wise and generous reader, mentor, model teacher and friend, heaps of thanks to Tom Fox for talking me through the rough patches.

Thanks to Lara Vetter, Kirk Melnikoff, and Thom Anderson for their friendship, encouragement, and support.

And, finally, thank you to Todd Lockhart, my heart.

AROUND THE TEXTS OF WRITING CENTER WORK

1

INTRODUCTION

*The Writing Center Journal's feature "Theory in/to Practice" (T/P)
offers writing center specialists a new venue for innovative work.
Like the more traditional academic essays that comprise the bulk of
the journal's contents, these works demonstrate an engagement with
recent research and contemporary scholarly debates. Unlike traditional
scholarly essays, however, T/P showcases those primary documents
that manifest the scholarship of our everyday practices—those syllabi,
annual reports, and other writing center documents that translate our
disciplinary expertise for an external audience.*

—"Call for Submissions: Theory in/to
Practice" (2010, *Writing Center Journal*)

Writing centers, by their very nature, experience high rates of turnover and, thus, are continually peopled by newcomers, both tutors and
administrators. With so many novices cycling through, and relatively
few long-time specialists with deep knowledge of the field, how does
a writing center develop and sustain a robust community of learners?
Through an analysis of an assemblage of everyday writing center documents and the activities that circulate around them, this book argues for
a variety of practices that work to build and maintain a writing center
learning community, firmly grounded in research and theory. Inspired
by the *Writing Center Journal*'s feature "Theory in/to Practice," this book,
addressed to both writing center administrators and tutors, demonstrates engagement with contemporary research and theory by show-
casing primary documents that manifest the scholarship of everyday
practices. Documents include a list of twenty valued practices for tutoring writing, excerpts from transcripts of tutoring consultations, samples
of session notes detailing the work of tutoring, posts and comments
from a writing center blog, and an assignment description for a tutor-
led inquiry project. The purpose is to illustrate the ways everyday documents both enact and forward writing center scholarship. Each chapter
includes background on a specific document and the exigencies that

DOI: 10.7330/9781607325826.c001

led to its creation and surrounding activities. The centerpiece of each chapter is the document itself. Then each chapter offers an analysis of the document, exploring its innovations, showing how it engages current scholarship, as well as how it enhances practices and extends, complicates, and offers new approaches to longstanding disciplinary challenges. These challenges include various aspects of writing center work, from tutoring to program assessment, all converging around an overarching concern—the tie that binds these documents together—tutor education. In addition to their preoccupation with tutor education, these focal documents and the chapters that analyze them are linked by two more key concerns: (1) a set of conceptual frameworks, which adhere to advance related principles for writing center work, and (2) an inquiry-stance toward writing center work.

CONCEPTUAL FRAMEWORKS

With this text-based approach to writing center scholarship, I argue for grounding the everyday documents we create, whether policy statements, websites, course syllabi, assessment plans, promotional flyers, annual reports, or the many other genres we engage to do writing center work, in conscious conceptual frameworks. With each chapter, my goal is to show the ways focal documents reflect and generate underlying assumptions about writing, teaching, and learning. Examination of everyday documents, I argue, illuminates the theories that underpin and motivate writing centers. As Nancy Grimm (2009) puts it, we need "a willingness to question foundational assumptions that typically guide writing center practice." Informed by George Lakoff, Grimm invites writing centers to examine the "unconscious cognitive models" we use to understand our work. This orientation is not mere navel-gazing. As Grimm points out, examining conceptual underpinnings invites change. "Significant change in any workplace occurs," she writes, "when unconscious conceptual models are brought to the surface and replaced with conscious ones" (16). This book takes up Grimm's invitation by applying a variety of theoretical lenses to everyday writing center documents to unearth the foundational principles that animate their creation and the activities that take place around them.

These theoretical lenses include the following: communities of practice, activity theory, discourse analysis, reflective practice, and inquiry-based learning. While these lenses are not new to writing center scholarship, bringing them together in this way sheds light on the ways these conceptual frameworks work as complimentary or adjacent theories to underpin tutor education. All the frameworks share fundamental understandings of teaching, learning, and writing as inherently *social* activities. All understand language use in terms of *action*. All are *dynamic*. In this way, the theories that animate each chapter do not operate together in absolute consistency, but they adhere to construct a consistent set of principles for writing center work, and tutor education in particular. To illustrate their usefulness for analyzing writing center documents, I've highlighted one as a primary analytical framework for each chapter. At the same time, I occasionally draw connections to one or more of the other theoretical perspectives. While one lens affords a certain view of a particular document, I encourage readers to explore ways that the other perspectives might also be applied in order to illuminate different aspects of a document and the activities that circulate around it.

Popular books for tutor training, such as Donald McAndrew and Thomas Reigstad's (2001) *Tutoring Writing: A Practical Guide for Conferences*, Ben Rafoth's (2005) *A Tutor's Guide: Helping Writers One to One*, Paula Gillespie and Neal Lerner's (2007) *The Longman Guide to Peer Tutoring*, and Christina Murphy and Steve Sherwood's (2011) *The St. Martin's Sourcebook for Writing Tutors*, tend to be practical rather than theoretical. Even texts that do address theory explicitly, such as Robert Barnett and Jacob Blumer's (2007) *The Longman Guide to Writing Center Theory and Practice*, do so narrowly, through the field of rhetoric and composition. With few exceptions, notably Nancy Grimm's (1999) *Good Intentions: Writing Center Work for Postmodern Times*, Elizabeth Boquet's (2002) *Noise from the Writing Center*, Harry Denny's (2010) *Facing the Center*, and Jackie Grutsch McKinney's (2013) *Peripheral Visions for Writing Centers*, writing center work remains under-theorized. For readers who ask, "Why this book now?" One answer is that there is a continued need in our field to theorize writing center work. That John Nordloff's *Writing Center Journal Article*, "Vygotsky, Scaffolding, and the Role of Theory in Writing Center Work," won the 2015 International Writing Centers Association (IWCA) Outstanding Article Award reflects this urgency. Nordlof (2014) addresses our field's "resistance to systematic or theoretical thought" this way:

> While our theories often lack empirical evidence to support them, they also do not function for us *as theories should* for a discipline. That is to say, the typical role of theory within a discipline is to provide a broad explanation of the processes that underlie the surface phenomenon that can be observed. In other words, theories provide the "why" to help us understand the "what." (47–48; emphasis in original)

That's my goal: to get at *a broad explanation of the processes that underlie the surface phenomenon* of the documents showcased in each chapter and the activities that surround them.

In my experience, however, many writing center professionals and peer tutors alike tend to resist "theory." They see it as abstract, remote, and removed from the practical business of tutoring. But I'm not interested in theorizing for theory's sake. Rather, as Nordlof (2014) suggests, theory is essential to understanding the "why" behind the "what" of our activities. Identifying the same aversion to theory in the wider field of composition, James Zebroski (1994) puts it this way in *Thinking Through Theory: Vygotskian Perspectives on the Teaching of Writing:*

> Theory—the word too often conjures up notions of the impractical, the superfluous, even the sophistic. Too frequently, compositionists have opposed theory to practice and have opted for practice, for "what works." But what do we mean when we assert that an activity "works"? How do we gauge apparent practicality? How do we evaluate the success or failure of a writing activity or our own teaching? The moment we begin to ask such questions, to reflect on our reflections, we are involved in theory. (15)

We can't sidestep theory. The "why" is always already present, whether we're conscious of it or not. My argument, to echo Grimm (1999), is to bring our "whys" to the surface for critical examination. To draw from Zebroski (1994) again:

> Theory is not the opposite of practice; theory is not even a supplement to practice. Theory *is* practice, a practice of a particular kind, and practice is always theoretical. The question then is not whether we have a theory . . . that is, a view, or better, a vision of ourselves and our activity, but whether we are going to become conscious of our theory. (15)

When I use the word *theory*, then, throughout this book, I refer simultaneously to its multiple meanings and functions, which are entangled: first, as Nordlof (2014) puts it, theory is *explanatory*. Second, theory is a *heuristic*, a tool of discovery and invention. Third, theory includes the *principles* that guide practice. Fourth, theory is the *unacknowledged or implicit values, assumptions, and beliefs* that underlie everyday routines. This fourth meaning is closest to Grimm's (1999) alternative term, "conceptual frameworks," which I use interchangeably with *theory*. I prefer Grimm's phrase because it forwards the image of underlying structural supports, like the beams that shore up a building. In this sense, conceptual frameworks are the foundational assumptions that determine how we act. Buried shallow or deep, again, they are always already there, whether we choose to investigate them or not. The challenge is to excavate our frameworks for careful examination to determine exactly *how* they organize and structure what we do. *Conceptual frameworks* also suggest a fifth function of *theory*, this time as a "frame" or "lens" through which to look. This metaphor draws our attention to both the affordances and the constraints of any framing device: none can encompass the entire picture. Rather, they all narrow and focus our attention to a *particular view,* allowing us to see some things while ignoring others. Conceptual frameworks, then, are tools for seeing and analyzing writing center work. Lauren Fitzgerald and Melissa Ianetta, in *The Oxford Guide for Writing Tutors: Practice and Research,* make a persuasive case for theorizing writing center work in their chapter "Looking Through Lenses: Theoretically Based Inquiry" (Fitzgerald and Ianetta 2015). Here they point out the ways that theorizing can provoke new questions and novel ways of re-seeing writing center work. For these authors, theorizing is not an end in itself. Rather, "we're concerned with the verb *theorizing,*" they write, "the actions associated with using theory, rather than with the noun *theory,* which would entail focusing on and explaining previously existing theoretical constructs." In this way, Fitzgerald and Ianetta argue, "interpreting and applying theoretical texts can be considered a research method" (212). This is the stance I take toward theorizing in this book, as a research method for unearthing the values, assumptions, and beliefs that inhabit and animate everyday writing center documents.

It's their everydayness, I think, that makes the mundane documents of writing center work so inviting for theoretical inquiry. Their ordinariness and ubiquity make them easy to overlook. At the same time, the theories that underpin the creation of writing center documents are also easily neglected. In *Science in Action,* Bruno Latour (1987) shows how a hypothesis or speculation either becomes a fact or remains merely a curiosity. He calls *fact* "ready-made" science—as in "already-made": it is "black-boxed," Latour says, certain, unproblematic, and stable, and it provides a foundation for future work. He refers to *speculation* as "science in the making" or "science in action": it is, Latour tells us, "rich, confusing, ambiguous and fascinating," and its future is uncertain (15). Your computer is one example of *already-made* science: its operations are taken for granted, certain. When you turn on a computer in the morning, you don't wonder *how* it works or *why* this way and not some other way; instead, you simply rely on it to get your other "work-in-the-making" done. By contrast, speculation is "science in action," ideas that are not yet "black-boxed," fixed, and certain. Latour's idea of "black-boxing" is a useful way to think about conceptual frameworks. We need, constantly, to take our frameworks out of the black box to name and critique them. For the more routine practices become, the less available they are for reflexive, critical examination and change. To get at the "why" beneath the "what" of writing center work, as Nordlof (2014) puts it, we need to put our theoretical lenses up for study.

While the frameworks in this book operate together to explicate many aspects of writing center work, like any frameworks, they are limited. With that in mind, we need to interrogate any writing center theory for its benefits and costs. We need to avoid allowing any perspective to rise to the level of dogma, turning the work of tutoring into rights or wrongs. Rather, we need to keep an eye out for gaps. Any theoretical perspective must be adopted with caution, with doubt. But to do writing center work effectively, we must have a coherent, conscious, explicit theory of teaching, learning, language, and literacy. In short, this book argues for a stance of openness and curiosity toward conceptual frameworks, the underpinnings of writing center work, and at the same time skepticism. The document-based exploration that follows, then, invites readers to reflect on theory and practice in a spirit of inquiry, looking for and carefully considering other frameworks beyond the few described in this book to support the work of writing centers. My applications of various frameworks for analysis, then, are intended as illustrations. I encourage readers to consider other theories too, which might better—or differently—serve your own purposes. After all, the shoe I use to pound in a picture hook may work just fine for me, but you may prefer a hammer.

AN INQUIRY-STANCE TOWARD WRITING CENTER WORK

In addition to theorizing writing center work, there is also a continued urgent need for research in writing centers. Calls for further and more rigorous research are not new in the field of writing center studies (Babcock and Thonus 2012; Driscoll and Perdue 2012 and 2014; Fitzgerald 2014; Gillam 2002; Grimm 2003; J. Harris et al. 2001; Lerner 2014; Neuleib and Scharton 1994; North 1987; Pemberton and Kinkead 2003; Thompson et al. 2009). But these calls have recently become louder and more insistent. Dana Driscoll and Sherry Perdue, for instance, point out that fewer than 6 percent of articles published in the *Writing Center Journal* between 1980 and 2009 include replicable, aggregable, and data-supported (RAD) research. In a recent follow-up study, they explore the reasons for this lack of RAD research. One problem is that "while we are collecting a lot of data," they point out, "over half of WC [writing center] administrators see that data only in terms of how it might be described to external stakeholders or upper administrators, not necessarily as data that can be used by the field to better understand its practices and to develop more data-supported best practices" (Driscoll and Perdue 2012, 117–18). A wealth of writing center data is bound up in a myriad of everyday documents, which cry out for study. But as Anne Ellen Geller and Harry Denny note, many writing center professionals do not view contributing to the scholarly conversation as central to their professional lives (Geller and Denny 2013, 118). Even among writing center practitioners who do value making scholarly contributions to the field, exigency, time, and resources to carry out research are often lacking, confounding the growth and development of knowledge making in writing center studies. Many writing center administrators, it seems, spend so much time designing and managing the documents that mediate writing center work that pursuing scholarly research projects too often takes a back seat or falls by the wayside altogether. One goal of this book, then, is to make a case for inquiry into everyday writing center documents in order to identify and analyze the theories that inform their creation and use.

Along with a push for more empirical research from writing center professionals, there is also a growing chorus of calls for more student-led research. Jackie Grutsch McKinney's (2016) new *Strategies for Writing Center Research* is a spirited and accessible methods guide suited to both seasoned specialists and novice student researchers. Likewise, *The Oxford Guide for Writing Tutors*, which includes a number studies authored by students, also reflects the move to valuing both RAD research and student voices in writing center scholarship. With this mission in mind, at a recent IWCA conference, Ianetta (2015) described her process of launching novice tutors into forming research questions and taking steps toward Institutional Review Board (IRB) approval during the first meeting of her tutor-education course for beginners. She was motivated, she explained, by her view that our field has not made enough space at conferences and in scholarly publications for research conducted by student peer tutors. A second edition of *The Oxford Guide* would contain an even higher percentage of student-led research, Ianetta promised. While I am happy to see this positive turn in the field, we need to take care to cultivate a culture of inquiry, with deep and sturdy roots, particularly among novice tutors, in which high-quality RAD research has adequate time to mature and flourish. Novices need to become acquainted with relevant conversations in the field before framing research questions. Research, for both novices and veterans alike, needs time to percolate. To that end, I propose a more gradual unfolding of inquiry, driven by some problem or question, which emerges out of sustained work in writing center research, theory, and practice over time. Thomas M. McCann

(2014), in *Transforming Talk into Text: Argument Writing, Inquiry, and Discussion, Grades 6–12*, directs us to John Dewy for a definition of *inquiry*:

> In *Logic: The Theory of Inquiry*, Dewey, (1938) defines *inquiry* in this way: "Inquiry is the controlled or directed transformation of an indeterminate situation into one that is so determinate in its constituent distinctions and relations as to convert the elements of the original situation into a unified whole" (pp. 104–105). I understand Dewey to mean that inquiry begins with the recognition of an area of doubt, an "indeterminate situation." This recognition leads to the expression of a question or questions (i.e., a *problem*) that set off an investigation or the purposeful seeking of a solution to resolve the doubt, at least by arriving at a tentative conclusion and by shedding some light on some areas that previously had been dim. The investigation relies on reasoning and the command of techniques, operations, or procedures that will support illumination. For Dewey, the inquiry process might result in something more "determinate." At the same time, inquiry into one question often triggers other questions and an inquiry cycle continues. (27)

One reviewer of an early draft of this manuscript posed the question, "What would your ideal tutor-education program look like?" Initially, I balked. That's not my project, I thought, to forward an "ideal." But, if pressed, I'd say that my ideal tutor-education curriculum would be animated by the spirit of inquiry valued by Dewey and McCann. But what does such a writing center culture of inquiry look like, exactly? This book aims to show readers, through the five focal documents and activities around which each major chapter is organized. As products of an inquiry stance toward writing center work, these documents emerged not as parts of carefully designed, formal research projects but as responses to persistent doubts and questions about tutor-education, which have emerged over time. The projects described here are, however, no less "research." With evidence gathered from a local writing center context, theoretically grounded methods of analysis, and involvement of peer tutors themselves, each chapter illustrates principles of inquiry-based teaching and learning. By first growing the habits of mind of an inquiry stance toward writing center work, I argue, tutors are then better equipped to develop primary research projects of their own, organically, not on demand. Drawing from and amending McCann's (2014) "features of inquiry," then, each chapter is bound together by the following features:

- A compelling **problem** or area of doubt, without a definitive, pre-scribed answer.
- **Data**, from both primary and secondary sources, including a **focal document or documents**.

- **Procedures of investigation,** explicit methods of gathering information and analyzing data.

- **Conceptual frameworks for analysis,** theories that illuminate the *why* behind the *what* and the *how* of writing center work, the underlying values, assumptions, and beliefs that shape practice.

- **Interaction with and among peer tutors** to build data sets, practice thinking strategies, and develop the habits of mind that characterize an inquiry stance toward writing center work.

- **Report of conclusions,** including creation of related assignments, activities, and products, as well as identification of new areas of doubt and further lines of inquiry.

- **Transfer and application,** putting inquiry-based discoveries to use in everyday writing center practice and applying the principles of inquiry-based teaching and learning to new situations. (27–28)

Because the documents vary in type and function, individual chapters do not lend themselves to a consistent, lock-step pattern of organization, which might be expected by the bulleted list above. Rather, I encourage readers to look for these features of inquiry as underlying principles, which are always present, but enacted and articulated with variation, and with different features foregrounded or backgrounded chapter by chapter.

WHAT TO EXPECT

Examined through the lens of "communities of practice," the focal document of chapter 2, "Valued Practices for Building a Writing Center Culture of Observation," is a list of tutoring practices, which serve as a rubric for observing tutoring. Writing center literature on observing, however, reflects persistent doubts about whether or not to observe in the first place. The presence of an observer, the narrative goes, changes the nature of the consultation, generating anxiety in both tutors and tutees. As a result, effective tutoring may be compromised. To avoid disrupting consultations, the literature suggests, administrators should sidestep observations altogether, opting instead for less threatening modes of evaluation, such as mock tutorials and participant observations. Underlying much of this conversation about observing is the assumption that its primary aim is summative evaluation of individual tutors. By contrast, this chapter details a three-year study of 163 observations, focused on formative feedback. Analyzed through the lens of communities of practice, at the center of this initiative is the primary document "20 Valued Practices for Tutoring Writing," which structures systematic observations, organizes program assessment, and prompts tutor education. Based on the use of this document, our analysis of data suggests that rather than avoid observations, or substitute them for inauthentic alternatives, we ought to make direct observations a centerpiece of our work. While we should not ignore observation anxiety, shifting the purpose from high-stakes individual evaluation to formative feedback and program assessment may reduce it. This enables a culture of observation, in which observations are no longer one-off occasions for high anxiety, but ubiquitous and central to program improvement, and especially tutor education.

Chapter 3, "An Activity Theory Analysis of Transcripts of Tutoring," draws upon Vygotsky (1978), Engeström and Miettinen (1999), and other leading theorists of cultural historical activity theory, including David Russell (1995), whose review of writing research, which makes use of activity theory, suggests implications for writing center work. With the primary document of the session transcription, this chapter shows readers how to locate the "moves" that tutors make—what work gets done and how—through an activity theory framework. This chapter demonstrates how tutors may apply this conceptual framework as a heuristic for working together with writers to learn the context for writing, including its motive, objective, tools, subjects, rules and conventions, community of practice, and division of labor. Teachers have lots of tacit knowledge about writing in their disciplines and about their particular expectations, which are rarely made explicit to students. Activity theory provides a framework for peer consultants of writing to determine what a writer understands about a specific situation for writing, and what more she needs to learn in order to accomplish her writing objective. In addition to its usefulness in helping to understand the context for writing, this chapter proposes that writing center workers consider the tutorial itself as an "activity system," examining, in particular, their role in it—and the ways their perspective of the activity may coincide or conflict with that of the writer—and with what consequences. To put it another way, as a framework for understanding and doing writing center work, activity theory is useful for unearthing both the context for writing and the activity of the tutoring session itself.

Examples of tutor reports, or session notes, are the featured documents in chapter 4, "Commonplace Rhetorical Moves of Writing Center Session Notes." According to James Gee (2005) in *An Introduction to Discourse Analysis: Theory and Method*, "Whenever we speak or write, we always and simultaneously construct or build seven things or areas of 'reality.' Let's call these seven things," says Gee, "the 'seven building tasks' of language" (11). These tasks include "significance," "activities," "identities," "relationships," "the distribution of social goods," "connections," and "sign systems and knowledge." Analyzing seven hundred notes from tutoring sessions, I examine how language builds reality in the writing center and what these realities tell us about tutors' underlying conceptual frameworks and identities. Studying session notes, I argue, can illuminate the social language of writing centers in general, and our own local writing center contexts in particular. As everyday artifacts of writing center work, excerpts from this corpus of session notes chart that social language, as they demonstrate the ways tutors take up—or don't take up—its situated meanings and patterns, become enculturated into that language, and adapt the genre to their own ends. Through the commonplace rhetorical moves enacted in session notes, tutors enact shared principles of the local writing center community of practice and construct identities, both for themselves and for the writing center as an institution.

Chapter 5, "Blogging as a Tool for Dialogic Reflection," showcases as its primary document posts and comments from an internal writing center blog to highlight the value of reflective practice among tutors. Engaging the long-standing scholarly discussion on reflective thinking and writing among writing center workers, this chapter argues that, to be more broadly useful for tutor education and professional development, reflections need to be shared in dialogue with other consultants. Such dialogic reflection is a powerful tool for tutor learning.

Chapter 6, "Problems of Practice: Developing an Inquiry Stance Toward Writing Center Work," takes as its primary document an assignment for a tutor-led inquiry project, which serves as the basis for ongoing tutor education for experienced consultants. Whereas a novice tutor-training course is designed and implemented by the writing center director, following that class, this inquiry project invites experienced consultants to determine for themselves what new questions about various aspects of writing center work to study. Grounded in the scholarly conversation about inquiry-based learning introduced here in the introduction, this chapter, like chapters 1 and 3, emphasizes collaborative learning among consultants to build a coherent writing center community of practice.

Guided by an inquiry stance and supported by data, this book seeks to contribute to evidence-based theorizing of writing center work, arguing for tutor education focused not merely on instrumental strategies, but on developing conceptual frameworks—habits of mind and critical lenses to inform writing center work. One way for tutors to learn writing center theory is to engage with authentic documents generated within a writing center itself. The mundane documents of everyday writing center work, like the focal documents of each chapter that follows, both reflect and create the conceptual frameworks that guide writing centers, and our design and implementation of tutor education in particular. To put it another way, the documents and associated activities that organize and structure our work are a "what" that cry out for further scrutiny of the theories that provide the "why" behind them. While novice tutors are especially eager for a bag of tricks—a set of how-to's for tutoring—when that bag runs out, consultants are left without principles and propositions for generating effective practice. By contrast, conceptual frameworks provide critical lenses with which to judge the effectiveness of writing center work—including everyday documents—and to invent an endless array of flexible practices-in-action. By examining key conceptual frameworks via analysis of the primary documents presented in each chapter, this book argues for a more conscious theoretical stance toward writing center work. That is not to say that theory is privileged above practice. Rather, the two are inseparable. The one is always informed by and informing the other. Writing center administrators and peer tutors alike always have reasons for working the way they do. The challenge is to make those reasons conscious, explicit, to call them up for examination and, perhaps, revision. Deliberate interrogation of our everyday writing center documents, I argue, is one way to do that, and thereby to engage in scholarship.

2

VALUED PRACTICES FOR BUILDING A WRITING CENTER CULTURE OF OBSERVATION

"All learned occupations have a definition of professionalism, a code of conduct. It is where they spell out their ideals and duties. The codes are sometimes stated, sometimes just understood."

–Atul Gawande (2009), *The Checklist Manifesto: How to Get Things Right*

IN THIS CHAPTER

- **Focal Document:** a list of "20 Valued Practices for Tutoring Writing"
- **Purpose:** to communicate a shared repertoire of tutoring strategies for observing, program assessment, and tutor education
- **Conceptual Framework for Analysis:** communities of practice
- **Data:** direct observations of tutoring
- **Assignment:** "Video Case Discussion"

Having directed two university writing centers over the past decade, I understood that taking on a new post leading the writing center at the University of Central Florida (UCF) would entail a period of transition, in which I would need to learn the lay of the land. In order to enter the culture of this new writing center, I would have to understand its work. To that end, I decided to observe consultations systematically over time. But I would have to step lightly, because observations, particularly from a new administrator and outsider, would almost certainly feel threatening. Before I began, and to foster buy-in, I asked a small group of peer tutors to make a list: "What would you want me to notice if I were observing your tutoring?" I asked. In addition to conducting my own observations, I invited two novice coordinators to observe. I hoped this activity would help them to learn the culture of their new surroundings as well. I also proposed that tutors themselves would observe one another repeatedly over time.

DOI: 10.7330/9781607325826.c002

IDENTIFYING VALUED PRACTICES

Now peer observing was already a routine in this writing center. But, based on a first round of written observation reports from consultants, I saw that they had no common agreements about *what* to observe for—or *why*. Tutors simply noticed whatever interested them. By contrast, shared principles and propositions for observing might lead us to unearth—and, perhaps, critically examine—underlying values and assumptions guiding tutoring routines. Likewise, deconstructing tutoring into specific subskills might lead consultants to practice those moves consciously and deliberately. My aim was to build on what consultants were already doing well—observing and noticing—but with the added dimension of noticing *specific practices*. With that goal in mind, I also asked consultants, "What would you want to see and hear when *you* observe other tutors at work?" As you make your list, I directed, focus on observable *actions*. To get the group started, I offered a couple of examples: "Establish rapport with the writer." That's something you can see and hear a tutor do. "Offer useful suggestions for revision." Over several weeks, consultants and I drafted and revised the list. They insisted on some practices I would not have thought of on my own. They debated practices, adding some, discarding others. Most importantly, consultants talked to each other and to me about tutoring. They wondered if some routines were peculiar only to themselves, or if they were generalizable to the entire writing center. Occasionally, practices outside the mainstream were proposed, but the wisdom of the crowd prevailed, prompting consultants to justify their choices, not only through their own experiences, but also via published scholarship in writing center studies. Consultants carefully worded each item on the list. Soon, we had "20 Valued Practices for Tutoring Writing," the focal document for this chapter. As you can see, for the most part, these practices would be recognizable to writing center workers anywhere.

WHY NOT "BEST" PRACTICES?

For a time, we called this list "best practices," but an annotated bibliography compiled by a graduate consultant led us to drop the moniker "best." Widely used in many professions, best practices are commonplace from business, to financial management, to medicine, to law, to education. The idea of best practices has recently gained some traction in writing centers (Graziano-King and Parisi 2011; Moberg 2010; Sherven 2010). Nevertheless, criticism of the concept is widespread (Christensen 2007; Coffield and Edward 2009; Feek 2007; Osburn,

Table 2.1. 20 Valued Practices for Tutoring Writing

Consultant: _____ Observer: _____ Date: _____ Time: _____

The following are some valued practices for effective tutoring, identified by UCF Writing Center peer consultants themselves. Write brief notes about what you see and hear. Then use your notes to offer formative feedback and to facilitate conversation between you and the consultant you observe.

	Tutoring Practices	Observation Notes / Formative Feedback	Assessment NR NP PNS PSS PHS
1	Establish rapport with writer.		
2	Learn assignment requirements or rhetorical situation, including the writer's understanding.		
3	Learn about writer's processes, beliefs, and attitudes toward the writing task.		
4	Set reasonable expectations and negotiate with writer what to work on and why.		
5	Address writer's learning beyond the specific task.		
6	Ask questions and use directives to engage writer in active learning.		
7	Address writer's concerns.		
8	Focus on only a few specific issues to work on in a single consultation.		
9	Prioritize global concerns that interfere with meaning before less significant local errors in grammar, punctuation, and mechanics.		
10	When addressing sentence-level errors, target selected patterns of repeated problems. Avoid a scattershot approach.		
11	Create opportunities for writer to demonstrate learning by talking, practicing writing strategies, and problem solving.		
12	Demonstrate active listening. Avoid dominating the conversation. Make effective use of wait-time.		
13	Offer specific, useful suggestions for revision.		

continued on next page

Table 2.1—*continued*

	Tutoring Practices	Observation Notes / Formative Feedback	Assessment NR NP PNS PSS PHS
14	Use, explain, and recommend writing resources, print and online.		
15	Work together with the writer to make a plan for next steps after the consultation. Sum up that plan in the session notes.		
16	Invite writer to return to the Writing Center; schedule a follow-up consultation.		
17	Use tone and body language to facilitate learning.		
18	Be a co-learner and collaborator. Engage in intercultural communication. Avoid roles of editor and authority.		
19	Model strategies to find answers and to solve problems. Be willing to say, "I don't know." Don't pretend expertise.		
20	After the consultation, write detailed session notes of work done and recommendations for what to do next.		
	Comments:		

Caruso, and Wolfensberger 2011; Petr and Walter 2005; Smith and Sutton 1999). Colin Irvine (2012), for example, characterizes best practices as "Orwellian" (395). Handed down by uninformed "administrative authorities/managers," with limited understanding of education, Irvine insists, best practices "undercut creativity" and obstruct genuine teaching and learning (390). Later, Irvine softens his stance a bit, conceding that "the idea of 'best practices' is not inherently bad." Rather, his complaint is with "a *system* that implicitly and sometimes explicitly insists that 'best practices' are not only the best right now in this particular time/space but will continue to be the best . . . down the road" (403). Such criticism of best practices stems from its originator, nineteenth-century industrial engineer, Frederick W. Taylor, known for "Taylorism," an approach to production efficiency aimed at breaking every task into small, simple segments, which can then be analyzed, taught, and replicated, assembly-line style. As Taylor himself put it, his goal was to find the "one best way" of improving efficiency of production in industrial settings (Kanigel 1997, 18). Emerging from this business model, best practices appear instrumentalist (i.e., behave this way, conform, or you are fired.) This is not the aim of our "20 Valued Practices for Tutoring Writing." As Terese Thonus (2014) reminds us, "The point of tutoring is to individualize instruction" (205). A ridged set of common practices cannot work for all. Tutoring writing is, and must remain, a highly inefficient teaching and learning activity, whose specific contexts, even within a single writing center, are so varied that we should not hope to find the "one best way." Rather, the primary goal of our list is to ask tutors to share their routines and to look for places of intersection, tutoring moves common to our particular writing center community of practice.

CONCEPTUAL FRAMEWORK: COMMUNITIES OF PRACTICE

Anthropologists Jean Lave and Etienne Wenger (1991) coined the term "communities of practice" while studying models of apprenticeship among West African tailors, Yucatec midwives, US naval quartermasters, supermarket butchers, and recovering alcoholics involved in AA. By observing these diverse groups, Lave and Wenger came to understand learning as *participation in collaboration with others on meaningful activities toward some common goal*. This conceptual framework is central to an inquiry-based approach to tutor education, which depends upon group collaboration. According to this view, learning is not something to be acquired, as in a body of knowledge, which one either has or doesn't have. Rather, *learning is participation*. And *participation is learning*. Communities of practice, Lave and Wenger suggest, have three characteristics. First, a community of practice includes a "domain of interest," a sphere of concern and capability. Second, a community of practice includes members who engage in common activities, interact, and learn from each other over time. Third, a community of practice includes, as Wenger (2006) puts it, "a shared repertoire of resources: experiences, stories, tools, ways of addressing recurring problems" (2). While we all belong to multiple communities—yoga class, a snowboarding club, the movie service Netflix, not all of these are "communities of practice." While movie buffs *do* belong to a community of sorts in Netflix, we do not interact and learn from each other while working toward some common goal over time. In addition to these characteristics, communities of practice have a history of shared goals, meanings, and practices. They constantly reproduce themselves as newcomers join the community, take up its practices, and, eventually, replace old-timers. In this way, communities of practice are dynamic systems. What's more, members maintain and transform the community as they adopt and adapt its practices; likewise, the community sustains and alters individuals through opportunities for participation and enculturation.

In *The Everyday Writing Center: A Community of Practice*, Anne Ellen Geller et al. (2007) offer the idea of communities of practice as a tool for analyzing writing center work. This chapter extends and complicates a communities-of-practice understanding of writing centers by examining the range of activities that take place around our "20 Valued Practices for Tutoring Writing." While much research is devoted to the learning between tutors and writers, comparatively little attention has been given to the ways in which consultants learn from one another. A communities-of-practice theory of learning focuses our attention on this important aspect of tutor education. In the context of our writing center, where experienced consultants, or mentors, play a central role in educating novices, a communities-of-practice framework is useful for understanding teaching and learning among old-timers and newcomers. Rather than focus on individual knowing or tutor development, then, a communities-of-practice perspective turns our attention to the joint activities—the shared *practice*—of the writing center, the transactional process of becoming enculturated into that community, and the resources, such as this list of tutoring practices, which mediate that process. Through this list, tutors take up, learn, and transform their community's shared goals, meanings, and practices.

One shared goal that links the "20 Valued Practices" is to prompt writers to demonstrate learning. For example, when tutors ask writers to explain their assignment requirements, this move engages writers in talk. The writer's talk is a demonstration of learning. By explaining to the tutor, the writer rehearses her own understanding, clarifying the rhetorical situation for herself, and perhaps identifying points of confusion or unanswered questions. Tutors could instead make it their habit to ask writers for a copy of the assignment, and then, to get an understanding for themselves, tutors could simply read silently to themselves. This move, however, leaves writers sitting passively on the sidelines, engaged not in learning, but in watching tutors learn. Identifying persistent moves that prompt writers to demonstrate learning has helped us to build a writing center community of practice based on explicit principles, which remain flexible, dynamic, and open to critical examination. This list, then, is a temporary "reification," only stable for now

(Wenger 1998, 57). To draw from Atul Gawande's (2009) *The Checklist Manifesto,* "[C]hecklists must not become ossified mandates that hinder rather than help. Even the simplest requires frequent revisitation and ongoing refinement" (183). This is a living document, not a sacred text, which we continue to discuss and revise in regular staff meetings, with new cohorts and shifts in our community of tutors prompting further revisions. While "best" implies the only/right way to tutor, "valued" acknowledges that these practices are not arbitrary or neutral. They are negotiated. They are privileged. Thus "valued" prompts us to confront the ways that power circulates in and around such a list. "Valued" invites questioning, such as "Valued by whom?," "Why?," and "To what ends?" "Valued" invites us to trace the ways our writing center community's shared goals, meanings, and practices evolve over time.

HOW TO READ "VALUED PRACTICES"

Before examining the list more closely, some guidance on how to read it. While items are numbered, the order does not intend a hierarchy or sequence of activities. This is not a step-by-step recipe for moves to make from the beginning of a consultation to the end. Although the first and last practices may imply a logical order, no sequence dominates; rather, with each diverse tutoring session, a different order of activities may be called for, with multiple practices enacted simultaneously. The "20 Valued Practices for Tutoring Writing," then, is not a checklist, in the sense of a rigid set of behaviors tutors must engage in lockstep order, but it does serve an important function of a checklist. As Gawande (2009) argues, checklists are useful to help manage complexity. But, he cautions:

> [U]nder conditions of true complexity—where the knowledge required exceeds that of any individual and unpredictability reigns—efforts to dictate every step from the center will fail. People need room to act and adapt. Yet they cannot succeed as isolated individuals, either—that is anarchy. Instead, they require a seemingly contradictory mix of freedom and expectation to coordinate, for example, and also to measure progress toward common goals. (79)

Initially, to avoid possible confusion about ordered steps for tutoring, I resisted numbering. But, over time, I gave in to repeated requests for numbers, because they facilitate ease of discussion.

As you can see, some practices concern observable behaviors tutors agree ought to be performed, such as "Use, explain, and recommend writing resources during consultations" and "Assist the writer to make a plan for work after the consultation." Other practices suggest roles consultants ought to play, such as "Be a co-learner and collaborator. Engage in intercultural communication. Avoid the roles of editor and authority." And "Model and explain strategies to find answers and solve problems. Be willing to say, 'I don't know.' Don't pretend expertise." Still other practices focus on the actions of tutees, such as "Create opportunities for writer to demonstrate learning by talking, practicing writing strategies, and problem solving." While this list will likely be familiar to writing center workers anywhere, what is innovative, I think, are the myriad of *activities* that take place around this document, including observing, programmatic assessment, and tutor-education. These activities, not the document itself, are the focus of the analysis that follows. But first, a review of the literature on writing center observations.

DOUBTS ABOUT WRITING CENTER OBSERVING

Writing center scholarship on observing tutoring reflects persistent doubts about whether or not to observe in the first place. The presence of an observer, the narrative goes, changes the nature of the tutorial, generating anxiety in tutors and even tutees (e.g., see Camp 2007; Devet 1990; Griggs 2012; Komara 2006). As a result, effective tutoring may be compromised. To avoid disrupting tutoring, writing center administrators should sidestep direct observations altogether, opting instead for less invasive, less threatening modes of evaluation, such as mock tutorials and participant observations (e.g., see Archer 1996; Griggs 2012; Komara 2006). Underlying much of the conversation about observing is the assumption that its primary aim is to evaluate individual tutors. This evaluative function is what makes observations so anxiety producing. Kirsten Komara's (2006) description is perhaps most striking in this regard. Under the subhead "Dramatizing/ Traumatizing the tutorial session," she writes, "My most anxiety-laden moment as a consultant was the time when my supervisor sat in on a consulting session" (12). Not only was Komara herself filled with dread, but also, worse still, the tutee himself fled the room because he too feared negative judgment. By contrast, Claudine Griggs (2012) is a bit more relaxed when her director comes calling: "I was not overly concerned," she recounts. "After all, I had two years' prior experience . . . I judged myself a competent tutor and felt self-assured about responding to a student paper under scrutiny." Even so, Griggs goes on, "I was acutely aware of being watched. Despite my confidence, I was nervous" (6). Similarly, Heather Camp (2007) explains that when the purpose of observations was understood by tutors as mainly evaluative, they "responded to them with indifference, annoyance, or dread," seeing them as "a policing mechanism or as a mandatory documentation practice" (4).

Negative perceptions about writing center observations have been forwarded by persistent comparisons to classroom evaluations and faculty annual evaluations. Darsie Bowden (1995) makes the connection this way:

> A . . . fundamental problem with observations and student evaluations is that both are inherently forms of assessment that are all too similar to the nerve-wracking evaluative systems already in place in the classroom. Classrooms are generally arenas where students' work is observed and assessed by teachers, and where teachers' work is observed and evaluated by students and/or superiors. Performance ratings go into permanent files used for graduation, contract renewals, merit pay, or tenure. (165)

Similarly, Griggs (2012) quotes from an editorial in *The Chronicle of Higher Education* to sew up the link between writing center observations and faculty evaluations: "As Ben Yagoda explains in 'Why I Hate Annual Evaluations' that he 'deeply and irrationally resent[s] being judged by a boss, I similarly resent being a boss who must judge. And the evaluation process itself, Yagoda writes, 'is undignified and unseemly.'" Her goal, says Griggs, is "to minimize the unseemliness" (8).

Efforts to minimize the unseemliness of observations include a variety of mitigation strategies. For example, Bonnie Devet (1990) recommends, "The best course for administrators is to ask if they may sit in on a specific tutorial. If the tutors are given the privilege of selecting the tutorial to be observed, administrators become partners, not foes in the evaluation." Alternatively, Devet suggests that administrators position themselves at a distance from the tutorial: "And with observers off to the side, incognito as it were, the tutors will be more relaxed as well" (8). By contrast, Maureen Archer (1996) reasons that sitting at a distance makes important aspects of the tutorial difficult to see and hear. Her remedy, like Komara's, is a mock tutorial, which she terms an "interactive exam." Archer explains, "To perform this assessment, the writing center director (or senior tutor) plays the role of interactor (inter + actor) dressing, acting, and reacting as a student in a tutorial. Immediately after the exam, the tutor and interactor discuss what they each perceived during the mock tutorial" (4). The problem with mock tutorials, however, is that they are not authentic representations of the complex, unpredictable, and endlessly variable activities of tutoring. Opting instead for something a little closer to reality, Griggs (2012) advocates that directors schedule authentic tutoring sessions to discuss their own writing with tutors. Harkening back to her own unpleasant experience as a tutor being observed, she explains, "To a large extent, I developed the procedure based on a desire to avoid formal client observations in a peer-tutoring center. I understood that my presence in a session (with notepad in hand) would almost certainly unsettle the most confident tutor" (6). Even with such mitigation strategies in place, however, the observation—whether authentic, mock, or participatory—is framed throughout the writing center literature as an activity whose primary purpose is to evaluate individual tutors.

REFRAMING THE PROBLEM: FROM SUMMATIVE EVALUATION TO FORMATIVE FEEDBACK

This framing is part of the problem itself. The narrative of anxiety, comparing writing center observations to high-stakes student assessments and faculty evaluations, has been crafted largely by writing center directors, who are themselves deeply enmeshed in the culture of academic evaluation. And so it is not surprising that we would frame writing center observations in terms of the familiar. What's more, persistent concerns about observation anxiety are a reflection of wider writing center values, which prize safe zones of comfortable, supportive relations above evaluation, whether between tutor and tutee or between writing center director and tutor. Just as tutors do not grade the writing of tutees, so directors would prefer not to evaluate tutors. Throughout the writing center scholarship, evaluation anxiety is a persistent worry, which must not be ignored. Psychologists Stewart Donaldson, Laura Gooler, and Michael Scriven (2002) explain:

> Most people experience anxiety when their behavior or achievements are being evaluated. Whether evaluations are formal, as in the case of standardized achievement testing, or informal, such as being picked to be part of a soccer team or cheerleading squad, the experience of being evaluated, critiqued, or judged commonly results in an emotional reaction of uneasiness, uncertainty, or apprehension. In essence, many evaluative situations cause people to fear that they will be found to be deficient or inadequate by others. (261)

Of course an observer changes a tutorial. And so observers must be mindful of our influence and strive to be as unobtrusive as possible (unless tutor and tutee invite us to become involved). But just because observations cause apprehension is not a reason to avoid them. There may be good reasons for occasional summative evaluations of tutoring. Even so, writing observations need not be kin to grading or tenure decisions. Rather, we ought to work to help consultants to make

their anxiety productive and to view observations as worthwhile learning experiences. After all, peer tutors are likely to go on to future jobs
in which they are frequently observed and evaluated. While the literature on observing has concentrated our attention wisely on the very
real and potentially disruptive consequences of observation anxiety,
this narrow focus has also caused attention blindness, preventing us
from seeing alternative possibilities. For instance, rather than fixat-
ing on *summative evaluation*, what if we viewed observations, instead, as
opportunities for *formative feedback*, whose primary goal is to facilitate
tutor learning?

Joe Law and Christina Murphy (1997) point out, however, that in
writing center contexts, conversations about formative assessment have
been largely absent: "[I]t is surprising, if not disturbing," they write in
a 1997 article, "to find that a search of the ERIC database for the terms
writing center, formative assessment, and their variants yields several
hundred entries individually, but the combined terms do not appear in
a single abstract or description." Two decades later, there has been no
change since the publication of their article. While, as Law and Murphy
point out, principles of formative assessment "[have] gone largely unacknowledged—or at least unnamed" their underlying assumptions have,
nevertheless, informed the conversation about observing tutoring (1).
For example, Roger Munger, Ilene Rubenstein, and Edna Burrow advocate an approach to observing that puts tutor learning as its primary
purpose, particularly for novices. "Initially, for the first two or three
weeks after our writing center opens," they explain, "tutors practice a
Chauncey Gardener-type 'I like to watch' healthy voyeurism by pairing
with veteran tutors in our writing center to observe tutoring nuances
such as body language, active silences, and questioning techniques"
(Munger, Rubenstein, and Burrow 1996, 3). Not only do tutors observe
one another at work, but also, more importantly, they discuss and reflect
at length on their experiences afterwards. In this way, novices accumu-
late multiple images of tutoring, while becoming socialized to the habits
of mind of reflective practitioners.

A PROTOCOL FOR WRITING CENTER OBSERVATIONS

This call for formative assessment in writing center observations
prompted a three-year study of 163 observations in our writing center. The conferences analyzed here and throughout this book were
part of multiple studies approved by the Institutional Review Boards
for Research Involving Human Subjects at California State University,

Chico, the University of North Carolina at Charlotte, and the University of Central Florida. Based on our findings, I propose that rather than avoid observations, or substitute them for inauthentic alternatives, writing centers ought to make direct observations a centerpiece of our work. While we should not ignore observation anxiety, shifting the purpose from high-stakes individual evaluation to formative feedback and program assessment may reduce it. Such a shift enables a culture of observation, in which observations, by both administrators and tutors, are no longer one-off occasions for high anxiety, but ubiquitous and central to ongoing tutor education and program improvement.

Popular tutor education texts such as Paula Gillespie and Neal Lerner's *The Longman Guide to Peer Tutoring* encourage observing, particularly for newcomers (Gillespie and Lerner 2008). As the authors put it, "GOOD OBSERVING = GOOD TUTORING." "We're convinced," they write, "that good tutoring starts with good observing, and as you gain experience, your powers of observation—and your ability to reflect on what you observe—will become some of your greatest assets" (72). If, as Gillespie and Lerner assert, "good tutoring starts with good observing," then writing centers ought to ask: what constitutes "good observing"? What do we look and listen for when we observe? And why? But writing center scholarship offers limited guidance. Gillespie and Lerner, for example, provide a helpful list of "reflective/analytical questions" for observers to ask, some of which imply effective practices, such as question posing, active listening, and agenda setting, but without necessarily naming practices explicitly. For instance, the questions "Did the tutor seem to respect the writer's work? How did she communicate this?" imply that tutors should, indeed, respect the writer's work and convey that respect to the writer (65). That's a practice consultants may demonstrate in a variety of ways. Other questions on Gillespie and Lerner's list, however, are more vague, inviting description, but without an indication of what tutors should *do*—and thus what observers should look for. For example, the question "How did the tutor end the session?" is an important one (66). But what, readers are left to wonder, makes for an effective ending? The value of keeping this question vague is that it asks us to observe with openness and curiosity, considering a wide range of possible ways to conclude a session. The downside is that Gillespie and Lerner give no indication of the kinds of practices that effective consultants engage in to conclude a consultation, or those practices that may make an ending problematic.

Without relational teaching practices to draw from, or images of effective tutoring in mind, novice tutors, in particular, are left to notice whatever interests them. As a result, they may fix on aspects of tutoring that may not be especially significant. For instance, though body language is meaningful, that a writer props his feet in a chair or hugs her backpack close during a consultation may be less important in our writing center's value system than, say, what those writers are *saying* about their writing or *doing* during the consultation to make revisions. But without shared values, tutors may witness a key decision point or move, such as inviting the writer to explain her assignment, without understanding its importance. By contrast, an observing protocol assigns value to particular routines. Our list, for instance, includes two specific moves that tutors said they valued as session enders: number 15, "Assist the writer to make a plan for work after the consultation" and number 16, "Invite the writer to return to the Writing Center, or schedule a follow-up consultation." Number 20 points to another specific session-ending move: "After the consultation, write detailed session notes of work done and recommendations for what to do next." Rather than guiding observers simply to describe how the tutor ended the session, naming particular practices gives us something specific to look for, reminding us of what our community of practice values. Using our list as a starting point, tutors can locate if a consultation achieved one of our ending goals, or if the session concluded in a way that seemed effective outside the boundaries of our document. In this way, "20 Valued Practices for Tutoring Writing" are not mandates we expect to see in every session. Rather, particularly in the learning context of our writing center, which includes a large number of novices discovering how to tutor for the first time, these practices are aspirational, learning outcomes for consultants themselves, what Shari Stenberg and Darby Whealy call "ends-in-view." Rather than rigid, predetermined outcomes, "ends-in-view," they explain, are "deserving of reflection . . . require a complex process of struggle, and whose results may not look exactly as we predict" (Stenberg and Whealy 2009, 704).

Our focus on explicit goals has helped us to transform the culture of observation in our writing center from noticing-whatever-you-notice to a systematic activity based on common agreements. One step in this direction has been to make observing frequent and routine, including observations by both peers and administrators. Unequal power relations between peers and supervisors, of course, necessitate differences in observing, about which I'll say more later. But regardless of who is doing the observing, as with practicing any activity, repetition promotes comfort. Also key to building a culture of observing has been a concerted effort to shift the focus from judgment and evaluation—the source of anxiety in much of the writing center literature on observing—to formative feedback. To that end, administrators approach observing much like writing teachers approach responding to students' writing. Writing teachers don't avoid response because we fear it might upset writers. We know that feedback makes writers apprehensive, and so, when we do it well, we temper criticism with praise. Likewise, rather than summative feedback, aimed at summing up a judgment, or justifying a grade, writing teachers put most of our energies into formative feedback, aimed at prompting writers to revise and improve over time. What's more, writing teachers commonly think of feedback not as a one-way transaction, but as dialogic, inviting conversation between responder and writer. In the same spirit of valuing formative feedback over summative evaluation, tutors in our writing center understand that observations are not high-stakes evaluations. This helps to diminish the counterproductive feeling that observations are a sinister means of surveillance, with dire consequences for those who fail to demonstrate proficiency. Rather, observations are opportunities to learn and to discuss what consultants are doing well, where they are having difficulty, and what they might do to improve.

For each observation, observers jot notes, and then follow with a short debriefing. In the case of debriefings with administrators, they serve as opportunities for relationship building between consultants and us. Most importantly, they work as concentrated opportunities for individualized instruction, in which tutors talk about their practices and speculate, not only about *what* practices they engaged in—or didn't—but, more important, *why*, and with what possible consequences. In debriefings, consultants and observers examine together various decision points, and then brainstorm alternatives for moving differently. They set goals—"ends-in-view"—for future tutoring.

Mindful of the disruption my presence as an observer may cause, I generally begin debriefings by asking consultants how they think I may have affected the tutorial. This gives tutors an opportunity to confirm that, yes, I made them nervous, or no, they hardly noticed me at all, or yes, my note taking *was* a distraction. My next prompt is usually, "Tell me what went well." In this way, I shift responsibility for evaluation from me to the consultant. While some tutors are vocal about their successes, others beat themselves up. When that happens, I point out what seemed effective to me. Rather than list defects in tutoring, I tend to ask consultants to reflect on their performance: "Tell me your reasoning for . . ." Our goal, then, in debriefings, is not to enforce rigid adherence to our list of valued practices but to use it as a springboard for explicating tutoring decisions. Here I am mindful of an important point made by Gawande (2009) about checklists: "The fear people have about the adherence to protocol," he writes, "is rigidity. They imagine mindless automatons, heads down in a checklist incapable of looking out their windshield and coping with the real world in front of them" (177).

In addition to moments of individualized teaching and learning, observation debriefings also act to reinforce common agreements across our writing center community of practice. For example, since so many of our tutoring practices highlight *learning* explicitly, during debriefings I typically ask tutors to point to evidence of the writer's learning. A focus on learning has gained attention in writing centers in recent years (see especially Bird 2012 and Geller et al. 2007). Our writing center takes its definition of *learning* from Ambrose et al. (2010), who remind us that "Learning is not something done *to* students, but rather something students do" (3). As a result of frequent conversations about learning, in both debriefings and our weekly tutor-education seminar, "Learning is doing" has become a sort of mantra in our writing center. Frequent observations and debriefings help to reinforce our shared understanding that although, as Ambrose and her colleagues point out, learning is a process that takes place in the mind, and so we can't actually *see* learning take place, we can, nevertheless, infer learning from what writers produce and *do*. By structuring observations around a set of shared principles, we've focused our collective gaze on learning-as-doing, asking, "What are tutors *doing* in consultations to prompt writers to engage in demonstrations of learning?"

A FOCUS FOR WRITING CENTER ASSESSMENT

In addition to structuring observations, this list of "20 Valued Practices for Tutoring Writing" also informs program assessment, which highlights a key difference between peer observations and observations conducted by administrators. In order to separate formative feedback from programmatic assessment, administrators wait until after debriefings with consultants to code feedback, using the designations in the right-hand column: NR = Not Relevant, NP = Not Present, PNS = Present but Not Successful, PSS = Present and Somewhat Successful, and PHS = Present and Highly Successful. Because these ratings are intended not to evaluate individual tutors but to learn how our writing center as a whole is—and is not— incorporating these practices, consultants do not see their ratings, only summaries of the data. Over six semesters, in addition to peer consultants' frequent observations and narrative reports about one another's tutoring, writing center administrators documented 163 observations of tutoring, with detailed notes concerning valued practices. Of course, initially we wanted to attend to all twenty practices on our list, but Ellen Schendel and William Macauley (2012) warn against this potential pitfall: "One mistake that newer assessment designers often fall into," they caution, "is the idea that they want to get as much out of each assessment as possible, and, as a result, try to do too much in one project." Instead, they advise, "*Choose a small number of goals you want to assess*" (Schendel and Macauley 2012, 31, emphasis in original). Because our list of twenty practices quickly becomes unwieldy, after an initial round of observations, we narrowed our gaze, for the purpose of programmatic assessment, to four particular practices. These were practices that three administrators conducting observations agreed were especially challenging for consultants—and frequently ineffective or absent altogether from sessions we observed:

#2 Learn assignment requirements or rhetorical situation, including the writer's understanding.

#4 Set reasonable expectations and negotiate with writer what to work on and why.

#9 Prioritize global concerns that interfere with meaning before less significant local errors in grammar, punctuation, and mechanics.

#11 Create opportunities for writer to demonstrate learning by talking, practicing writing strategies, and problem solving.

Figure 2.1 illustrates the success of these four focal practices over six semesters. First, we converted the lettered rankings to a numerical scale, 0–3. Thus, a score above two signals the presence and general effectiveness of a particular practice.

Here you can see that, over time, we have seen gains in all four areas, based on observations. Importantly, however, this data does not chart a neat and tidy narrative of progress, from struggling to demonstrate specific practices, to intervention, to ongoing success. Rather, as novice tutors are added to our staff each semester, while experienced ones graduate or go on to other opportunities elsewhere, we see an ebb and flow of practices. While we saw initial gains in tutors addressing writers' learning, for example, those gains dipped again with a new cohort the following semester. This ebb and flow may suggest not only that newcomers are learning practices for the first time, but also that experienced consultants, too, need frequent feedback in order to reflect on their practices, discuss them, and continue to develop and improve. In short, some practices are gaining a foothold, while others are emergent.

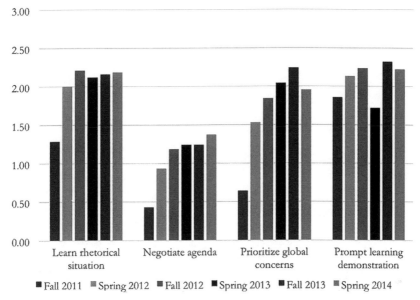

Figure 2.1. Four Troublesome Tutoring Practices for Program Assessment

Among other things, we wondered if the differences this data shows over time are statistically significant. Table 2.2 illustrates results of simple linear regressions, with each practice as a dependent variable and time (semesters) as an independent (explanatory) variable. *b* is the slope of the straight line that depicts the relationship between time (semesters) and ratings on each valued practice. They are interpreted like this, using the first valued practice, "establish rapport," as an example: we expect ratings for establishing rapport to increase by 0.08 every semester on our 0–3 rating scale. The strongest relationship is an expected increase of less than a quarter of a point per semester, so these are subtle positive trends. But *p*-values < 0.05 (the shaded tutoring practices) indicate that positive linear trends are statistically significant. The 0.05 indicates that there is a 5 percent or lower chance that we'd see these results by random chance (i.e., if there weren't actual trends at play here). Overall, then, over the six semesters of observations represented here, we see statistically significant positive trends for half of our "20 Valued Practices for Tutoring Writing." In other words, our analysis shows that we can be fairly confident that consultants as a group are enacting these practices more effectively over time. For the non-significant practices, we still get *b* values, but we can't be sure they're statistically different from 0. In bold are the four troublesome focal practices.

Table 2.2. Statistical Significance

#	Valued Practice	b	p
1	Establish rapport	0.084	0.043
2	**Learn rhetorical situation**	**0.065**	**0.058**
3	Learn writer's processes	0.225	0.001
4	**Negotiate agenda**	**0.124**	**0.009**
5	Address learning/development	0.141	0.004
6	Ask questions, use directives	0.031	0.396
7	Address writer's concerns	0.1	0.01
8	Focus on a only few issues	0.173	0
9	**Prioritize global concerns before local**	**0.15**	**0.002**
10	Avoid scattershot approach to errors	0.123	0.088
11	**Prompt writer to demonstrate learning**	**0.025**	**0.533**
12	Use active listening, shared talk	0.098	0.023
13	Offer revision suggestions	0.059	0.101
14	Use and explain writing resources	−0.03	0.534
15	Assist in making a plan for after the consultation	0.014	0.763
16	Invite writer to return to the WC	−0.021	0.686
17	Use tone/body language to facilitate learning	0	0.993
18	Avoid role of editor/authority	0.153	0.003
19	Don't pretend expertise	0.156	0.003
20	Write useful session notes	−0.001	0.981

Shaded   Statistically significant
Bold   Four troublesome tutoring practices

Further analysis of the data, including a statistical technique called an exploratory factor analysis, led us to look at different variables (valued practices, in this case) and identify how they group together in the data. This is illustrated in table 2.3. Here, columns, or categories, are composed of practices that "hang together" statistically. In other words, if a consultant got a high rating on learning the rhetorical situation, then he probably also got high ratings on negotiating an agenda, addressing the writer's concerns, and so forth in the same column. Conversely, consultants who struggled with one of those practices tended to struggle with the others in the same category, as a general trend.

These groups also seem to group together thematically, and so I added a heading at the top of each column to convey my sense of each

Table 2.3. Explanatory Factor Analysis

Organize the Work	*Involve the Writer*	*Teach Instead of Tell*	*Make the Writer Welcome*
Learn the rhetorical situation	Learn writer's processes	Address learning/ development	Use tone/body language to facilitate learning
Negotiate agenda	Ask questions, use directives	Use and explain writing resources	Write useful session notes
Address writer's concerns	Prompt writer to demonstrate learning	Avoid role of editor/ authority	**Establish rapport**
Focus on only a few issues	Use active listening, shared talk	Don't pretend expertise	**Invite writer to return to WC**
Prioritize global concerns before local			
Avoid scattershot approach to errors			
Assist in making a plan for after the consultation			
Offer revision suggestions			

theme. The practices in each column fit statistically significantly into the model, except for the three practices in bold. I suspect that's because two of them (establishing rapport and offering revision suggestions) are things that peer consultants do in almost every observation, whereas inviting the writer to return is something almost every consultant forgets. I added these practices into categories I thought they might fit with conceptually, to include them in the categorization scheme. Together, these categories suggest relationships among tutoring practices, and, perhaps, that we ought to work to teach them explicitly as groups or categories of related moves.

While observations are commonplace in writing centers, particularly newcomers observing veterans, we've learned that observations, in and of themselves, are not inherently productive. For example, when I asked one peer tutor, after an observation, why he chose to read a paper silently, while the writer moved to a computer at another table to check his e-mail, this tutor explained that he read silently because that's what he'd observed an experienced consultant do during his first weeks as a newcomer. Debriefings like this one highlight that communities of practice have a history of shared goals, meanings, and practices. They constantly reproduce themselves as newcomers join the community, take up its practices, and, eventually, replace old-timers. While reading a paper silently may be productive in certain circumstances, in a writing center context, too often this routine leaves writers sitting passively on the sidelines, disengaged from learning. And so we generally discourage this practice. Nevertheless, in a writing center, as in other communities of practice, routines such as this one are forwarded with each new generation. While tutoring practices are by no means uniform now in our writing center, our list of valued practices has helped us to name, if not common codes of conduct, then assessable principles for tutoring. Coding data from observation reports has led us to identify strategies consultants find most difficult, and to keep them at the forefront of our collective attention and tutor education over time. By naming what we value, and by including consultants in the negotiation and revision of these practices, we've developed an assessment plan that reflects the values and priorities, not only of writing center administrators, but also of peer consultants themselves.

GUIDING PRINCIPLES FOR TUTOR EDUCATION

Key to making this assessment meaningful has been to follow another piece of advice from Schendel and Macauley (2012): "*Integrate what you have learned into your program, completing the feedback loop*" (emphasis in original, 32). For us, integration has meant revising our approach to tutor education and training. After our first round of observations, this data helped us to identify problem areas for consultants and to redesign tutor education to address those tutoring practices explicitly. We could see, for example, that consultants often struggled to negotiate an agenda with writers or neglected to make a plan altogether. Over time, this remains a challenging practice. This, in turn, leads to what Beth Hewett (2010) terms a "scattershot" approach to tutoring, in which consultants simply target whatever catches their attention, without a clear sense of purpose or core priorities for the writer's learning (85). Without an explicit agenda, tutors focus too quickly and narrowly on correcting sentence-level errors in grammar, punctuation, and mechanics, rather than first tackling global concerns of content and organization. Without clear priorities for the session, consultants also neglect to assist writers to make plans for what to do in revision after consultations. With a limited focus on the writing at hand, rather than on the writer-as-learner, consultants give little attention to the writer's development beyond a specific writing task.

As teachable moments, debriefings, it turned out, proved as illuminating as the observations themselves. In our writing center, they have become key opportunities for tutor education. Initially, novice consultants, in particular, reported the same challenge of particular valued practices: "I understand that this is something I should do, but I'm not sure what it *looks* like, exactly." "I know *what* to do; I just don't know *how*." As Muriel Harris (2006) reminds us, "the *what* and the *how* of tutoring are very different." Tutors may understand and agree with specific principles that underlie tutoring. They may even include them in a list of valued practices. But "the *how*, the strategic knowledge" for putting those theories into practice may be unclear (Harris 2006, 303, emphasis in original). If learning is *doing*, then how, newcomers wondered, might they prompt a writer to "demonstrate learning?" How would we know a *demonstration of learning* when we saw one? Debriefings prompted us to see that novice tutors need more strategic knowledge.

But for experienced consultants, the same disconnect between stated values and actual tutoring practices may require a different explanation. According to Chris Argyris (1991), we operate via a "theory of action—a set of rules that individuals use to design and implement their own behavior as well as to understand the behavior of others. Usually, these theories of action become so taken for granted that people don't even realize they are using them." A paradox in human behavior, says Argyris, is that our "espoused" theory of action—the theory we *say* guides our behavior—often contradicts our actual "theory-in-use"—the theory that determines how we *actually* behave (7). Repeated conversations with tutors suggested to me that this contradiction was operating among experienced tutors. In order for tutoring to become more effective, in addition to providing more strategic know-how for new tutors, we also needed to help long-time consultants to bring their espoused theory of tutoring—their list of tutoring practices—into alignment with actual tutoring behaviors. A first step was to learn the reasons for the contradiction. In their debriefings, consultants repeatedly recounted feeling pressured to give writers what they wanted, even if what they wanted didn't reflect shared tutoring principles. If a writer wanted a tutor to rush to proofread and edit for her, ignoring content altogether, then consultants felt forced to comply. By contrast, naming goals for tutoring urged consultants to shift motives, to put the writer's learning above merely "fixing" or "getting through" a paper.

With new information about what consultants found challenging, we redesigned tutor education. The four tutoring practices consultants consistently named and demonstrated as most challenging became learning outcomes for the following semester. We selected readings that addressed these four practices directly, helping to reinforce them as valued beyond our individual writing center. We assigned consultants to observe one another repeatedly, isolating each practice in turn. We asked consultants to consider three questions as they observed, and to write and talk about these questions in weekly seminar:

- *How* do you see and hear tutors enact the practice—or not?
- What is challenging about the *how* of this tutoring practice?
- What *alternatives*—including outliers—for working can you imagine?

We also selected readings in writing center research and theory to target each practice. For example, articles such as Muriel Harris and Tony Silva's "Tutoring ESL Students: Issues and Options" helped to reinforce specific tutoring practices, such as agenda-setting and prioritizing global concerns before local, even as the authors complicate distinctions between the two. Harris and Silva (1993) acknowledge the tension consultants experience when attempting to negotiate priorities:

> ESL writers often come to the writing center seeking an editor, someone who will mark and correct their errors and help them fix the paper. On the one hand, as tutors, we are collaborators who listen to the student's concerns when setting the tutorial agenda. On the other hand, as tutors we also want to begin with rhetorical concerns before looking at sentence-level matters. This causes delicate negotiating between tutor and student when differing preferences for the agenda collide. But tutors should be firm about dealing with rhetorical matters before linguistic ones. (530–31)

While these authors urge a "firm" stand on prioritizing, others, such as Nancy Grimm (2009), advocate a more flexible approach. As she puts it in "New Conceptual Frameworks for Writing Center Work," "Within the framework of Global Englishes, a writing center needs to develop new ways of responding to requests from novice users of English who want help 'proofreading' their papers. The consequence of not proofreading is politically significant, and in the context of linguistic bigotry it is unfair to simply deny the request" (18). One persistent complaint about the notion of "best practices" is that they are not evidence based (Osburn, Caruso, and Wolfensberger 2011, 217). This criticism prompted us look to writing center scholarship to support each practice on our list. We also sought out moments of dissonance like this one, the various and sometimes-conflicting ways writing center professionals discuss the same practices. In the case of proofreading, for instance, we decided that prioritizing global concerns *before* local does not mean ignoring requests to proofread; rather, it means making a deliberate and strategic decision about *when* (not *if*) to address proofreading. Some writers do need their usage addressed, and may stick around to learn other things, once they become convinced that a tutor is listening and responding to what they perceive their needs to be. Rather than sidestep requests for proofreading, consultants may engage writers in conversation about the politics of language use and the ways language changes, depending on context, purpose, and audience.

On the one hand, reading writing center literature with specific practices in mind, again, draws attention to the fact that there is nothing new about our list of valued practices itself. If that is so, then that's a good thing, suggesting that our local common agreements are also common across writing centers more broadly. As Dana Driscoll and Sherry Perdue point out, however, there is a tendency among writing center administrators to emphasize our differences over our similarities, yet, as in the case of observations for tutor education, their findings "revealed quite similar discussions and activities taking place in diverse writing centers" (Driscoll and Perdue 2014, 121). Writing center communities of practice, then, in spite of our many differences, are not islands. We do share some commonplace valued practices. At the same time, reading our list of practices through the writing center scholarship also reminds us that these principles do not speak for themselves. Rather, with each new cohort of consultants, tutoring practices require repeated interpretation, and, with experience, reinterpretation. As Wenger (1998) reminds us, practice, even when it is shared, "does not itself imply harmony or collaboration." Communities of practice "are not privileged in terms of positive or negative effects" (85). Nevertheless, our list of practices has helped to turn our attention to the joint activities—the practices—of our writing center, the transactional process of becoming enculturated into that community, and the resources, such as observations and debriefings, which mediate that process—what Wenger terms the "shared repertoire" of experiences, stories, tools, and ways of addressing recurring problems (82).

Before observing systematically, I knew that tutors' talk about their work was often far afield from what actually happens in consultations. In the tutor-education course, in particular, I could see that tutors often become adept at talking about writing center research and theory in ways that make them appear as confident and effective tutors. But I knew, too, from many individual conversations with consultants that this was not necessarily the case. Mostly, I dismissed this misalignment as inevitable, a part of tutors' learning processes. But now, by making observations a centerpiece of our work, I can see more clearly what's actually happening in tutoring, and I can be more effective in helping tutors to align actual practices with stated principles. Jackie Grutsch

McKinney (2013) calls for just this sort of move in *Peripheral Visions for Writing Centers.* She urges writing center professionals to engage less in storying about our writing centers and to look more closely at the work that actually takes place there (80). Frequent observations, conversations, and reflective writing about those experiences have led us to examine our "shared repertoire" of resources more closely, and the stories that develop around them, unearthing not only what is challenging about the *how* of tutoring, but also what strategies consultants see and hear that prompt writers' learning, and the strategic knowledge consultants need in order to put those strategies into practice. Our focus on named practices has not yet brought espoused theories of action into complete alignment with theories-in-action, but they have helped us to identify where the two contradict, where to intervene to bring them closer together, and where to challenge common agreements and question shared routines. This is particularly evident, for example, around the value of setting expectations and negotiating what to work on and why. While some tutors have become adept at making plans with writers early on about what priorities to tackle and in what order, others skip agenda-setting and rush ahead to read and respond to the paper, without first establishing learning goals. Still others tutor somewhere in the middle, with learning goals and agendas arising only after lengthy conversation about the text in question.

COMPLICATING AND EXTENDING TUTOR EDUCATION

The activities that take place around our "20 Valued Practices for Tutoring Writing" have helped to prompt meaningful, collaborative change in UCF's Writing Center. We've learned that observations are useful, but equally important are the conversations they prompt. With common agreements in mind, because consultants observe one another often, they talk to each other frequently, in person in the break room between consultations and on our blog, about specific practices. Tutors also write and share reports and reflections about their experiences, both observing and being observed, which leads them to reflect on and develop practices further. Through these peer-to-peer learning activities, tutors prompt themselves and one another to explain and to justify tutoring moves and decisions. Recognizing that informal dialogue about observations is as valuable as the observations themselves, consultants recently called for a poster version of our "20 Valued Practices" to hang on the wall of the consultant break room, where the most significant learning among tutors takes place. Further research on the talk around observations might unearth what values—not only valued practices, but also values about academic writing, about teaching and learning, about professionalism, and so forth—are revealed in these conversations.

A key intervention in our revised tutor education has been to make peer-to-peer observations routine and to make the writing about and discussion of those observations central to weekly tutor-education meetings. Jane Van Slembrouck (2010) comes to the same realization, pointing out that observations by administrators alone sidestep valuable opportunities for consultants to learn from one another. As she explains, observations by administrators

> felt somewhat disconnected from the center's dynamic social habitat wherein tutors routinely confer with one another between and even during sessions, asking questions, and suggesting resources. Suspecting that at least some of this productive exchange disappears when the director comes calling, I wondered how to reduce my role in the evaluation process and find a means of assessment that would take advantage of this nonhierarchical flow of ideas. (2)

Van Slembrouck's solution is a process of peer observations. With our list of tutoring practices, this has been our aim as well. But the key is not just in the *using* of the list but also in the *making* of it. After all, I could simply have made a list of tutoring practices myself, without involving consultants. But that list would have been truncated, reflecting only my own limited values alone. What's important about the list is that consultants themselves participated in its creation and subsequent revisions.

Readers, then—and this is critical—should not simply take the list presented here and distribute it in your own writing center. My point is that the document itself is not the "thing." Rather, the activities we engage in *around* such a list, including observations, assessment, and tutor education, are what truly matter. The activity of generating the list in the first place, together with consultants, facilitated communication, trust, and learning—for both consultants and administrators. Again, this is a living document, subject to further change. Each semester, and with each new cohort of consultants, our articulation of tutoring practices continues to evolve. After putting them to the test for a time, consultants are invited to reflect on them, critique, and revise them. Some ideas are added; others fall away. Over time, some practices have been combined, while others have been teased apart. Some practices have fallen away altogether, while others have been added. This participation and negotiation is where learning takes place, and where our writing center is becoming coherent as a community of practice.

Because its creation and revision are distributed among consultants, our "20 Valued Practices" build and reflect the consensus of the group. That is not to say, however, that differences are ignored or smoothed over because, at the same time, the list prompts writing center staff to negotiate dissensus, to accept sometimes uneasy disagreements. Even among practices that elicit strong collective agreement, differences prevail. For example, no one would argue that rapport building is unnecessary. We can all agree that this is a practice that, ideally, ought to be enacted in every consultation. Or can we? Some nonnative speakers of English, for instance, may not respond well to the chit-chat that commonly begins a session between native speakers of English, preferring, instead, to get right to work (Muriel Harris, email message to author, December 14, 2012). If tutoring practices are so arbitrary, then, why try to list them in the first place? Perhaps tutoring circumstances are too varied to make such a list useful. But I don't think so. In our experience, the value of this list has been in its creation and in its repeated explication. After all, even the most obvious-seeming practice is demonstrated differently across consultations. Examining practices over time—placing how we actually act in the world against explicit principles of behavior—gives us ways of understanding that behaviors can change because they are socially and historically situated (Lil Brannon, email message to author, June 11, 2013). To return to building rapport, for instance, after moving to a newly-renovated space, in which our reception area is now across the hall from the main area in which tutoring takes place, consultants have debated not only if building rapport is appropriate for every consultation, but also what it should look like, where and how it should take place. As Gawande (2009) argues of checklists, "There must always be room for judgment, but judgment aided—and even enhanced—by procedure" (79). With that in mind, some tutors step across the hall to wait for arriving tutees, greeting them in the reception area, engaging in small talk while they guide writers across hall. Other consultants wait in the tutoring area, taking a moment to get acquainted only after the tutee has found his way and is seated for a consultation. Tutoring practices, then, invite multiple interpretations, which may comfortably inhabit the same writing center. What matters is not only the practice itself but the dialogue around it. This is central to a community of practice approach to tutor education. That talk prompts us not only to explain and to justify tutoring decisions, but also to make them public, open to question, debate, and further revision. Such talk considers, among other things, that our writing center includes multiple sites, including regional campus locations, with student and tutor populations that differ from one site to another. Given these varied contexts for learning, a one-size-fits-all (or a "one best way") approach to tutoring is not possible or even desirable. While we may agree on most practices most of the time, a change in learning context may warrant a change in tutoring practices, or at least a shift in emphasis. Our experience teaches us, then, that any list of tutoring practices needs to be flexible and responsive to its particular context.

Likewise, procedures for observing, too, need to remain flexible and open to experimentation and revision. To return to Thomas McCann's (2014) principles of inquiry-based teaching and learning, "The point of entry into inquiry is raising doubts about subjects and issues that the learners care about" (25). That means remaining open to doubt, even about well-established practices, such as observing. With that in mind, I end this chapter with another document, an assignment description that we developed after six semesters of observing, based on doubts expressed by tutors, who called for more control over the process and greater attention to following up on insights gained from observations and debriefings. To address the first concern, more control in the hands of tutors, we devised the Video Case Discussion assignment so that they could video record consultations of their own choosing, then select what, if any portion, to share for examination in our weekly seminar. To address the second concern, follow-up, we made this an explicit focus of small-group discussions of selected video clips. Having tested this assignment for only one semester so far, it is in its early days and, thus, premature to draw any meaningful conclusions about the usefulness of video case discussions. While we continue to conduct direct observations of tutoring as described above, this alternative seems to open new possibilities for examining and reflecting on tutoring practices, building on an already well-established culture of observation and inquiry-based learning. In particular, the "Video Case Discussion" assignment makes use of collaborative inquiry groups, in which tutors construct knowledge from examining and questioning their own practice and looking closely at the work of peers. As Alexandra Weinbaum et al. (2004) put it, "Collaborative inquiry groups are a vehicle for fostering . . . professional development. These groups are based on the notion, common to other professions such as medicine or law, that experts and novices learn from cases presented by their peers" (17). This sort of case analysis is the basis of this assignment.

ASSIGNMENT: VIDEO CASE DISCUSSION

Based on insights about observing developed during seminar last spring, this semester let's try a new practice of video recording and discussing tutoring sessions. For this assignment, you'll work in groups of three to four; this group will be your "video case discussion team." For experienced consultants, this assignment will temporarily replace observation reports as you've written them in recent semesters. As the semester unfolds, we'll reflect periodically on ways to revise and improve this new assignment.

Step 1: Record

Each individual in the group should check out a camera to record at least two consultations this semester, one during the first six weeks, and another during the second six weeks. (To avoid a mad rush of recording at the last minute, each group will be assigned specific weeks to record, so that all groups are not recording at the same time. (See the Canvas Webcourse list under your seminar day/time.)

Remember first to ask the tutee's permission, and then complete and sign an "Informed Consent" form before you record.

Step 2: Select

First, review your own video in its entirety. Then, choose a relevant five to seven minute segment of your consultation to view with your group by noting the timestamp for the duration of the segment.

Option 1: Select a clip based on your own questions about your tutoring practices.

Option 2: Select a segment to focus on one or more of the following troublesome tutoring practices listed below. (We've selected these because, based on recent data collected from observations, they are the most frequently absent among our twenty valued practices):

- When addressing sentence-level errors, target selected patterns of repeated problems. Avoid a scattershot approach (10).
- Assist the writer to make a plan for work after the consultation (15).
- Use, explain, and recommend writing resources, print and online (14).
- Set reasonable expectations and negotiate with the writer what to work on and why (4).

Step 3: Upload

To submit your video for seminar, paste the URL into the Video Case Discussion Assignment on our secure Canvas Webcourse site.

Step 4: Discuss

After you've recorded at least one consultation and selected a segment of interest, arrange to meet with your video case discussion team to view your clips and discuss. Be sure to allot enough time to view and discuss each consultant's video clip.

Watch your clips together, considering the following questions:

- Studying your video, what do you *learn* about your tutoring practices that you didn't know before seeing yourself in action?
- What tutoring *decisions* do you see yourself making?
- What seem to be some *consequences* of those decisions for the writer?
- How might insights gained by studying your video inform your tutoring *going forward?*

Take notes during your group discussion that you can reference during your follow-up discussion post and seminar presentation.

Step 5: Follow-up

After your group's discussion, generate a written record of your conversation, summing up your insights, plans, and suggestions in a brief post to the Canvas discussion board. You may write a single collaborative post and/or individual posts. If you write a group post, name all your group members explicitly so that everyone gets credit.

Questions to address:

- Based on your group's discussion, what do you intend to do differently during future consultations?
- What insights can your group offer to revise and improve any aspect of the video case discussion assignment?

Step 6: Present

From your group's multiple recordings, which you've viewed and discussed, now choose one or more brief video clips to show during seminar. Keep the video portion short (five to seven min. total), so that you have more time for the main event: thoughtful, in-depth discussion. A good clip for seminar is one that generates lively discussion about specific tutoring practices and decisions. Your goal is to facilitate *learning* among consultants through talk about your selection.

Sign up for a time to show your group's selection during seminar and lead a twenty-five-minute conversation about the video *and* your experiences talking together about it with your video team. Work together as a group to present. To prepare, your group should design a quick-write prompt or a couple of discussion questions to focus and guide the conversation.

3

AN ACTIVITY THEORY ANALYSIS OF TRANSCRIPTS OF TUTORING

"Rather than learning before acting, as traditional theories prescribe, activity theory believes a priori that the human mind emerges and exists as a special component of interactions with the environment, so activity (sensory, mental, and physical) is a precursor to learning" (64).
—David H. Jonassen and Lucia Rohrer-Murphy (1999), "Activity Theory as a Framework for Designing Constructivist Learning Environments"

IN THIS CHAPTER

- **Focal Documents:** excerpts of transcribed tutoring sessions
- **Purpose:** a tool for analyzing tutor talk and its consequences for learning
- **Conceptual Framework for Analysis:** activity theory
- **Data:** transcripts of audio recordings of tutoring
- **Assignment:** "Collaborative Activity Theory Transcript Analysis"

The previous chapter examined the document "20 Valued Practices for Tutoring Writing" through the conceptual framework of "communities of practice." One insight that this analysis brings to the fore is the extent to which this list of aspirational tutoring practices works to enculturate peer tutors into common activities, interacting, and learning from each other over time, via a shared repertoire of experiences, stories, tools, and ways of addressing writing center work. As I noted in the introduction, novice tutors, in my experience, are eager to know the "right way" to tutor, a formula for engaging a writing consultation. But no such formula exists. As helpful as a list of shared practices may be, it is no panacea. Sometimes particular valued practices aren't appropriate. Sometimes they don't work. What is more valuable for novice tutors are multiple opportunities over time to develop critical habits of mind that encourage them to reflect on practices in the moment, then, when tutoring isn't working, to innovate new, more effective strategies, based on a sound theory of teaching and learning grounded in research. To

DOI: 10.7330/9781607325826.c003

that end, rather than a recipe for how to tutor, writing consultants need a variety of robust tools for analyzing writing center work. This chapter offers activity theory as one such tool or another conceptual framework. While it is a useful heuristic for explicating any writing center activity, including observations, the tutors I work with have found activity theory especially illuminating for examining transcripts of recorded tutorials, the focal document for this chapter.

ACTIVITY THEORY AS A TOOL FOR ANALYZING TRANSCRIPTS

In recent decades, research in literacy instruction has demonstrated that teaching writing apart from the context in which it functions is to risk what Lynn Tamor and James T. Bond term "pseudotransactionality" (Tamor and Bond 1983, 99). As Joseph Petraglia (1995) and others have pointed out, when students experience writing as pseudotransactional, they view it as purposeless because it is displaced from the work it does in the classroom or in the world beyond (19). By contrast, an activity-systems approach to writing instruction invites students to consider the ways genres function in particular contexts. In this chapter, I explain activity theory, examine its intersection with research into novice learners' problem-solving practices, and show how to use this theory and research to explicate the activity of tutoring. Building on the insight of Joanne Hardman and Alan Amory that pedagogy may be understood as an activity system, (Hardman and Amory 2015, 10), this chapter draws upon Vygotsky (1978), Engeström and Miettinen (1999), and other leading theorists of cultural historical activity theory, including David Russell (1995), whose review of writing research, which makes use of activity theory, suggests implications for writing center work (51). With the primary document of the session transcription as its centerpiece, this chapter shows readers how to locate the moves that tutors make— what work gets done and how—through an activity theory framework. This lens, I hope to show, illuminates both the activities of writing and the activities of tutoring.

Writing center researchers routinely collect transcriptions of consultations to investigate various aspects of tutoring. Magdalena Gilewicz and Terese Thonus, for example, use transcripts to conduct conversation analysis in order to understand how patterns of talk shape the work that gets done in a consultation (Gilewicz and Thonus 2003, 40). Coding transcripts, Isabelle Thompson and Jo Mackiewicz detail a method of close, empirical analysis of experienced tutor talk (Thompson and Mackiewicz 2014). Neal Lerner (2007) mines transcripts for evidence of "situated learning" (53). While researchers such as Mary Rosner and Regan Wann have pointed out the limitations of transcription data, these documents remain a rich source for understanding at least some of the work that gets done in writing center consultations (Rosner and Wann 2010, 7). In our writing center, tutors regularly audio and video record consultations, transcribe them, and then analyze the data via multiple frameworks, including discourse analysis and activity theory. In addition to using them to analyze patterns of talk and evidence of learning, we use transcripts to explicate the activity system of the consultation. This chapter demonstrates how tutors may apply this conceptual framework as a heuristic for working together with writers to learn the context for writing. Because teachers have lots of tacit knowledge about writing in their disciplines and about their particular assignment expectations, which they may not always make explicit, contexts for writing are often initially unclear to students who visit a writing center for help. Activity theory provides a framework for consultants to determine what a writer understands about a specific situation for writing, and what more she needs to learn in order to accomplish her writing objectives. In addition to its usefulness in helping to understand the context for writing, this chapter proposes that writing center workers consider the tutorial itself as an activity system, examining, in particular, their role in it—and the ways their perspective of the activity may coincide or conflict with that of the writer—and with what consequences. To put it another way, as a conceptual framework, activity theory is a useful tool for inquiring into both the writer's context for writing and the activities of tutoring itself.

FRAMING THE PROBLEM: DOUBTS ABOUT TUTOR "EXPERTISE"

One strand of thinking about peer tutoring might be characterized as the knowledge-based approach. Work by Jean Kiedaisch and Sue Dinitz is one instance of this view, in which the emphasis in the debate over the role of disciplinary expertise among writing center tutors has been on what the tutor knows—or doesn't know. After analyzing one transcript, the authors tell us of their research subjects, "David doesn't seem to know what to do to move Anna beyond plot summary" (Kiedaisch and Dinitz 2001, 263). By contrast, "Tami knows not only what the disciplinary conventions are but also what process produces a paper that follows them" (268). Similarly, the focus of Alexis Greiner's (2000) advice for tutors is, first and foremost, based on *what the tutor knows*: "At some point, every consultant must recognize when the knowledge gap is too wide and the writer needs to be referred back to the professor for help. The knowledge gap can be a problem even when the consultant and writer are in the same field" (85). More recently, Sue Dinitz and Susanmarie Harrington, building on this previous research, make a compelling case for a long list of benefits that result when tutors leverage disciplinary expertise to shape the work of peer consultations (Dinitz and Harrington 2014, 93).

But suppose we examine the notion of expertise from an alternative perspective? As the examples above illustrate, the debate over whether writing center tutors require disciplinary expertise is based on the assumption that knowledge is individual and private. This assumption leads us to ask, "What does the tutor know about writing in the discipline, and how does she convey her understanding to the writer?" This is the "banking model" of education, or what Andrea Lunsford (2003) calls the "writing center as storehouse," which "operates as an information station or storehouse, prescribing and handing out skills and strategies" (48). By contrast, Stephen Toulmin's (1999) approach to activity theory challenges the conception of the individual as independent thinker and tutor as storehouse of disciplinary expertise:

> All . . . units of understanding obtain their meaning by entering language not via the minds of single individuals but within "forms of life" . . . that are essentially *collective*. As a result, the origin of any individual's questions and judgments is defined by the current state of the art in the relevant field of inquiry . . . So, . . . we find ourselves facing an important scientific question: "How is it, then, that individuals can be successfully socialized, or enculturated into the shared [knowledge] of any particular culture or profession?" (55; emphasis in original)

This question speaks directly to the intersection among activity theory, disciplinarity, and genre; it also motivates recent research in science, engineering, business, medicine, and other fields in which researchers are examining the ways that novices begin to understand and work in unfamiliar disciplines.

CONCEPTUAL FRAMEWORK: ACTIVITY THEORY

First, a brief explanation of activity theory. Activity theory concerns object-oriented, collective, and culturally mediated human activity or systems of activity. It is just that: a model—or theory—of human activity. Its central premise is simple: as Yrjö Engeström and Reijo Miettinen explain, all human activities include the following constituents:

- an activity, something to do, an "object," "objective," "outcome," animated by some "motive"

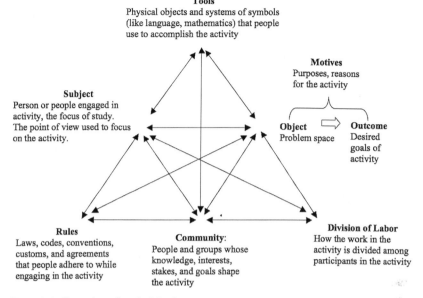

Tools
Physical objects and systems of symbols
(like language, mathematics) that people
use to accomplish the activity

Motives
Purposes, reasons
for the activity

Subject
Person or people engaged in
activity, the focus of study.
The point of view used to focus
on the activity.

Object
Problem space

Outcome
Desired
goals of
activity

Rules
Laws, codes, conventions,
customs, and agreements
that people adhere to while
engaging in the activity

Community:
People and groups whose
knowledge, interests,
stakes, and goals shape
the activity

Division of Labor
How the work in the
activity is divided among
participants in the activity

Figure 3.1. Illustration of an Activity System

- people who engage in the activity, participants, or "subjects"
- "Tools" for accomplishing the task
- "Rules," "conventions," or "customs" that govern the activity
- a "community" of people, beyond the immediate participants, who engage in the activity
- "Division of labor" among participants (Engeström and Miettinen 1999, 9)

To write—or to engage in any other activity, for that matter—we must enter into a complex web of human behavior, an "activity system." Figure 3.1 is Engeström and Miettinen's depiction of such a system.

Applying this model to a writing center context, tutors can be viewed as "subjects," learning collaboratively about writing alongside writers in order to achieve an outcome—the nature of which I will discuss as this chapter unfolds. Outcomes may include, for instance, successful completion of a writing task. "Motives" or "outcomes" may also include, for the writer, comprehending the subject matter in a particular course, learning common patterns of development in a discipline, and, for the tutor, understanding the teaching and learning of writing itself. "Tools" for achieving these outcomes may include, for example, assignment instructions, model texts, style guides, and handbooks. "Tools" also include the talk and gestures of writers and tutors. (Importantly, people are *not* tools in an activity system. They may, at times, feel used, as one might use a tool, but, as active participants, people remain only in the "subject" position or the "community" position in an activity system.) "Rules" may include the conventions for writing in a discipline, course, and even for a particular instructor. "Rules" may also include, for the consultant, commonplace tutoring practices such as guiding the writer by questioning, rather than providing answers. For the writer, "community" may include participants in the discipline for which he is writing, such as his teacher and classmates. A commonplace source of tension arises in a consultation when the consultant is not a participant in the writer's discipline or community. I argue that the consultant's expertise in the discipline is, in any case, beside the point in the context of many writing center sessions. With training in literacy teaching and learning, the consultant belongs to the community of writing tutors and teachers, though, again, relative expertise in this area will often *not* provide a means for structuring or guiding the work of the consultation. Regardless of their familiarity with the various disciplines they encounter in the writing center, from an activity-systems perspective, consultants are members of a writing center community of practice, learning the work of tutoring. This community includes both the local and the broader field of writing center studies. "Division of labor" in a writing center consultation may include, among other things, the writer's explanation of her understanding of the writing assignment, the teacher's description of the assignment, and the tutor's suggestions for interpreting the assignment. Activity theory is a useful heuristic for analyzing the work and these constitutive parts of a tutoring session. With practice, its principles and propositions may guide consultants not only to reflect on their effectiveness afterwards, but also to make effective decisions during a consultation.

THE ROLES OF TUTORS IN THE ACTIVITY
SYSTEM OF A PEER CONSULTATION

An activity theory approach to writing center work prompts us to reconsider the work—or activity—of the tutoring session, and the role of the tutor in that activity. Any activity the consultant and tutee undertake together will be structured by a set of possible activities available to them. Even a consultant well versed in the discipline from which the student's writing assignment comes is usually not a participant in the particular course in which the assignment is situated. One can imagine a consultant with knowledge of a field reading into an assignment a set of goals that the instructor may not intend. While disciplinary knowledge on the part of the consultant may be valuable, it is not enough; if the success of the session depends on what the consultant knows, then she must also understand the particular classroom context of the student's assignment. But, as Mary Broglie (1990) reminds us, tutors—even if they could be experts—cannot take the place of classroom teachers: "[T]he tutor, unlike the teacher," Broglie writes, "is neither the authority in charge who gives directions and determines what will happen nor an evaluator who indicates where a paper met or failed to meet acceptable criteria" (283). Muriel Harris (2001) defines the role of the tutor as "co-learner," "a hybrid, somewhere between a peer and a teacher, who cannot lean too much one way or another" (284). For Harris, the role of the "specialist" tutor is troubled. "[T]he more skilled tutors are," Harris cautions, "the further they are from being peers in a collaborative relationship. Students who see the tutor as a knowledgeable insider . . . want answers from the tutor, and a common problem tutors face is straining against telling students what to do" (282).

But if consultants are not going to adopt the role of *expert*, if they are not going to tell writers what to do about the tasks that writers find daunting and difficult, what meaningful activity *can* a consultant and student writer undertake that will benefit a developing writer? Although the tutor is not the teacher, she may attempt to behave like a teacher. She shares with the student the motive or desire of wanting the student to complete the assignment successfully. The goal of the session, then, can easily become narrowly text focused, rather than attending, more broadly, to the writer's learning. Activities may include correcting surface errors, providing and implementing rules for writing an introduction, for example, using evidence, following particular formats, and so forth. The consultant may determine that the student is confused about the assignment, and will try to set the student straight.

TROUBLING THE ROLE OF TUTOR "EXPERT"

In the following transcript excerpt, the consultant adopts this teacherly mode. I selected this excerpt—and the others that follow in this chapter—to illustrate key aspects of the activity system of tutoring. But any transcript will do. Any transcript can be read through the lens of activity theory. Study participants quoted and discussed throughout this book have been given pseudonyms. Here the writer, Wacey, has been assigned to critique a scholarly article and then to draw connections between the article and key concepts studied in an anthropology course. This and other transcript excerpts in this chapter follow the conventions of "vertical transcription" recommended by Gilewicz and Thonus (2003). As a result, transcripts may at first appear wonky to unfamiliar readers, because speaking turns are not neat and tidy, as they might appear in a conventional play script, with each turn simply following the previous one. By contrast, vertical transcriptions are intended to be read both left to right and up and down, or vertically. The unconventional spacing throughout is designed to show where speakers interrupt one another and where speech overlaps.

Transcript Excerpt 1—Wacey and Eric:

WACEY: Am, I mean, am I supposed to put "I think that" or "in my opinion," like in, can I use it that way, by saying, "In my opinion, I think"?

ERIC: I think it's asking for your opinion, um, and what you want to do—

WACEY: Basically, I'm, in the article, I'm for it. I don't really say it. I mean, should I say more like "in my opinion, I think that?"

ERIC: Yeah, I think that what you're, what you're struggling with is where your words are going to start and where the article's words end. Cause I think what you said earlier is that you feel that you're summarizing again,   and I think that if you look at the

WACEY: Mhmm

ERIC: areas that you feel that you're just summarizing again, it might help you out, um, cause after, um, the summary, let's see, I think you had it—

WACEY: Oh, another thing, what, um, um, like format and stuff are you supposed to use? Cause he didn't really be specific about what he wanted, so it doesn't really matter what kind of writing style or anything like that.

ERIC: I think he's got it set up here (3 sec.) [reading the assignment instructions]. He says, "introduction," "summary of the article," "your opinion of the article," and then a "conclusion."

From this point in the consultation, several pages of transcript reveal that Eric expounds on MLA format, even though, as it turns out, Wacey is not required to use that format in his paper.

This segment is crowded with issues. Wacey's confusion about his instructor's assignment expectations doesn't daunt Eric, who moves forward with some fairly definitive statements about the writer's problems: Wacey doesn't, in Eric's opinion, see where to place his own evaluation of the article and where to use summary of the article. When Wacey, who gives no sign of understanding this insight, breaks in with questions about format and style guidelines, Eric plunges into this territory as well. Both of them seem to be looking for something concrete to say and do, whether it's separating evaluation from summary, identifying format requirements, or examining the assignment again. Without quite saying that the writer has got the assignment wrong, the consultant conveys misgivings about the writing and wants Wacey to go back to his work in order to check his own tendency to summarize. In this part of their exchange, the consultant's response is characterized by a quest for answers, for prescriptions, if you will, to fix what ails the paper. Eric seems in search of an expert's role, a space from which he can speak definitively about the assignment, the student's writing, or both.

But from an activity theory perspective, tutors understand that what a student knows about writing is less important than what she will *do* with it—the *activity* or literacy practices his assignment calls upon him to enact. Although consultants like the one in this segment often speak with authority, their reflections on sessions tend to contain a high degree of self-doubt. While examining post-session reflections written by consultants in our writing center, I am struck by the number of times tutors write the words "I don't know" or "I wish I knew. . ." Consultants describe not knowing everything from what an assignment required, to what a teacher expected from a student-writer, to whether or not a session helped the student in any meaningful way. They often find it impossible to evaluate a session, and frequently give a session high marks if their interactions with a writer seemed mutually gratifying. While this level of confusion seems highly problematic at first glance, I became interested in imagining it as *necessary*. Given that consultants are not experts, that student writers are not experts, and that both are grappling with a problem given to the student writer in another setting entirely, it should come as no surprise that deciding what to do in a forty-five-minute consultation creates uncertainty. And because tutors genuinely want to help, when they feel they haven't, they can feel personally disappointed in their abilities as tutors.

LEARNING PROCESSES OF NOVICES

Writer and consultant must, however, do something, and given the inherent difficulties of working with writing outside of the context in which it arises, I became interested in the problem of describing what that "something" could or should be if we take activity theory into account. An intriguing insight comes from a chapter by Aviva Freedman (1995). While investigating how students learn to write in the disciplines, Freedman notes that

> Discovery procedures are ill understood and mysterious; insights come
> to us in the shower or in the middle of the night, in ways that we cannot
> explicate or replicate. Further, according to recent psychological work
> on experts and novices, such discovery procedures differ for experts and
> novices, so that even if we could model our own processes, it is not clear
> that it would benefit our students. (134)

Freedman writes here, tantalizingly, of a space where novices have their
own necessary learning strategies, which experts neither use nor tend to
understand. This, it seems, is territory worth investigating, since a writing center is arguably peopled with novices, both consultants and student writers, struggling to collaborate on strategies that would help writers learn everything from how to formulate meaningful questions about
specific writing assignments to how to write and evaluate their writing in
a range of unfamiliar disciplinary settings.

Studies on expert and novice practices in problem solving from the
fields of science, medicine, physics, and business have led me to view
peer writing consultants as *expert novices*. This term describes a remark-
able paradox of writing center work: while peer tutors cannot be literacy
experts or disciplinary experts, there is an area of experience that they
know well, if they can be brought to reflect on it and work within it consciously. That area is the world of the novice learner. Novices, according
to researchers John Smith, Andrea diSessa, and Jeremy Roschelle, tend
to exhibit the following three reasoning strategies:

1. Seek deeper explanations of the causality involved in situations than are
   immediately and superficially apparent.

2. Attend extremely selectively to features of situations, ignoring (abstract-
   ing from) many surface feature to focus on what they consider causally
   relevant.

3. Apply principles that (a) apply hypothetically to a given situation, (b)
   are intended to identify underlying causal mechanisms (deep structure), and (c) may be withdrawn under consideration of other arguments. (Smith, diSessa, and Roschelle 1993–1994, 131)

Novices struggle when encountering new concepts and practices, according to these researchers, in part because—unlike experts, who have
mastered an array of concepts in a field—they hold tenaciously to misconceptions that often cause them to attend selectively to the wrong or
limited features of situations initially. In a writing center consultation, for
instance, a student may cling to the format requirements of an assignment because he has the work of writing confused with mastering the
surface features of text (because commonsense and years of schooling

have taught him that surface-level correctness matters most in writing). Novices struggle as well, however, because of forms of instruction, which regard misconceptions as worthless, in need of expunging. Smith, diSessa, and Roschelle (1993–1994) critique what they term a "confrontational model" of teaching, which seeks to replace a novice's "naive understanding" of a concept or practice with a more sophisticated one (131). The problem with such an approach is that learning builds upon learning; by contrast, a constructivist, activity-centered theory of learning understands the students' pre- and misconceptions of a field or an activity to be a *necessary prerequisite to more complex or refined understandings.*

MAKING ROOM FOR MISCONCEPTIONS

At their best, then, writing centers offer a valuable learning activity, distinct from the classroom, not strictly disciplinary, but an activity about the learning processes of novices, about how learning takes place. With this in mind, a later segment from the same consultation with Wacey and Eric illustrates something closer to what I see as a productive learning activity of a writing center session.

Transcript Excerpt 2—Wacey and Eric:

ERIC: Now everything you read, you don't have to agree with, you know that, right?

WACEY: Yeah, but it's just easier to agree.

ERIC: Yeah, but it's not always necessary or easier to go that way with the reading. [Wacey laughs.] Cause sometimes when you have to agree with something that you don't really agree with it's harder in the long run, especially when you end up having to write a paper about it. Cause if you always have those hesitations in your head, then you might end up thinking, well, you know, maybe I'm going about this the wrong way.

WACEY: But doesn't that mean that the article is good, but maybe the research didn't—

ERIC: And I think that's what he's really asking for. The good or bad, good or bad of the article. (4 sec.)

WACEY: Okay, so it's basically more about, okay, well, I see that now. Plus it's going to be my opinion anyways, so whether he agrees or not, it   doesn't matter. As long

ERIC: Exactly.

WACEY: as I have   evidence to back it up.

ERIC: I think that's what—   That's exactly right.

This second segment, which occurs more than halfway through the session, begins with Eric's question, or forced agreement ("you know that, right?"), about the process of agreeing or disagreeing with the article Wacey has read. He says that it's easier to agree with a published article, a notion that the consultant troubles by asserting that it isn't always easier, and that false agreements with experts can lead to trouble later on in one's learning and writing processes. This is a conversation of an entirely different order from that in the first segment. Here the consultant does not tell the student that it *isn't* easier to agree with published sources, but that *sometimes* agreement does not work out. This provides Wacey with room to pit two concepts against each other: the first, that the published authority is most likely right; the second, that there is room for his own ideas about the article. This second concept destabilizes the first concept enough for Wacey to realize something new about the learning goals of his assignment: the instructor may, in fact, be interested in his opinion as a reader. To use the language of the novice learner research cited earlier, the student's initial misconception—that the published text is authoritative and therefore it would be best to agree with it—can be weighed against a new, more complicated possibility—that he needs to demonstrate understanding of the article, but that he does not necessarily need to agree with its methods or its conclusions.

It is precisely this second kind of interaction that writing center peer tutors are, I would argue, ideally positioned to have with the writers who come to them for help. An expert in the discipline would be unlikely to wade through the student's confusion to the underlying misconception that causes him to mistrust his own views. An expert in literacy studies might focus too quickly on the assignment, its context, and genre conventions. The peer consultant, however, after making some initial attempts to offer expert help, comes to realize that a crucial misunderstanding blocks the writer from exploring and writing about his own views. As a peer, Eric can ask Wacey about his misunderstanding without threatening Wacey's self-concept; indeed, he can find the misunderstanding precisely because he enters into the conversation from the stance of not-knowing, of wondering, of questioning what the writer is doing and why. Together, Eric and Wacey construct an alternative position available to Wacey but previously unseen, the position of critical reader. As Smith, diSessa, and Roschelle (1993–1994) would predict, the misconception itself is the key to helping the student move forward as a learner, not by identifying and then robbing him of it, but by allowing him to hold it as valid in some cases while simultaneously inviting him to explore another, competing possibility.

These two ways of doing the activity of tutoring suggest implications for tutor education. First, the knowledge-based model of tutoring, though persistent because of the commonsense idea that if one knows more, one can be a better tutor, ignores how novices learn and what activities support that learning. Second, in constructing tutors as *expert novices*, we can design training opportunities which invite them to reflect on *how* they have learned to write in an array of unfamiliar settings: what confusing situations did they encounter, what questions and encouragements supported their learning, what misconceptions did they come to reconsider? How might tutors use talk and scaffolding to help learners add new conceptual possibilities to the models of writing they currently hold? The tutoring session, then, isn't about giving knowledge—or even making it—so much as it is about discovering what a student knows and what she doesn't yet know about a particular context for writing, and what she needs to learn in order to write effectively.

TROUBLING TUTOR PRIOR KNOWLEDGE

An activity-theory analysis of another consultation illuminates the ways a consultant's prior knowledge may impede effective learning. Here, Vince, in his second semester as a peer tutor, brings his prior knowledge of writing studies research and theory to bear in his writing center work. The consultation we'll look at, however, shows that using what he knows about analyzing rhetorical situations to engage the writer to draw upon and expand what she knows is much more challenging. In this consultation, Vince is working with a sophomore, Denise, who is drafting a brief essay to include as part of her application for admission to our university's undergraduate journalism degree program. In the opening minutes, Vince asks for the prompt, then reads it aloud: "Submit a one-page typed essay that explains why you want to major in Journalism and that describes your career plans. The essay should not contain any grammatical or factual errors." As this session unfolds, a tension becomes clear: Denise and Vince have conflicting ideas about the rhetorical situation and the requisite genre of the application essay. For Denise, the prompt invites what she terms a "story" about how she was inspired to become a journalist. By contrast, Vince sees the situation as calling for an evidence-based argument, in which the writer works to convince readers that she should be admitted to the program. Vince is also certain that Denise's essay should highlight specific experiences that make her well qualified. But instead of telling Denise directly that he doesn't share her view of the essay's purpose, throughout the session, Vince tries to lead her indirectly to adopt his approach. Initially, Denise just wants Vince to read her draft. He resists, opting, instead, for her to talk through her answer to the prompt. She then tells him about her experiences writing for her high school newspaper. She also details a stint shadowing a public relations professional in a local sheriff's department. "Now," says Vince, "I'm going to ask you the big question: Where do you write about all this in your application essay?" "That was the hard part," replies Denise, "because it's only one page. But I did write about my inspiration, Christiane Amanpour, a journalist who works for CNN." Hearing what he perceives to be a gap between what the prompt asks and Denise's essay, Vince tries another activity. He asks Denise to take a few minutes to outline her draft, summing up the main idea of each paragraph. His purpose, Vince tells her, is "to understand the moves that you're making in your essay." But even after they discuss the outline, the impasse persists. Here's an excerpt from this point in the transcript:

Transcript Excerpt 3—Denise and Vince:

VINCE: [Reading from the prompt] "Why do you want to major in journalism? What are your career goals?" That's something that I want you to focus on. Bring that out more. Focus on your experience, because your experience actually is valuable. (3 sec.)

DENISE: I just felt like I needed to elaborate, because I didn't just want to just put out my, uh—

VINCE: What is your overall goal for this paper? (5 sec.)

DENISE: Hmm. My overall goal? Hmm. (2 sec.) I guess I just want this paper just to be, you know, a knockout, so that way I could make the cut for, because it is a limited-access program. So I just want it, you know, to stand out, I suppose.

VINCE: O.K., instead of "making the cut," why don't we reorient that, and think about not just "making it," but persuading the reader that you are a strong candidate for the program. Does that make sense?

DENISE: O.K., yeah, I understand what you're saying.

VINCE: Why would we be interested in doing that?

DENISE: Like, because, you don't want to bore readers. You don't want them to think that you're just, like, doing this because there isn't any other option for you. You know, like, "Why are you even here?" You want to keep the reader entertained. You want 'em to know that you're a human being.

VINCE: And those are nice things to add, but I want you to think about it differently now. This essay is doing some kind of work. And it's not— yeah, it's about entertaining and making sure you're a human being and whatnot. But it's trying to convince the audience. So what are some things that you would want to see in an application essay yourself, let's say, if you were a reader?

DENISE: (2 sec.) That I would want to see?

VINCE: Yeah, if you were on the admissions committee for a second, what would you like to see in an essay?

DENISE: Yeah, O.K., um, uh, gimme some time here (2 sec.). Um, as long as, like, you know, why you want to major in journalism, I think, uh, if the essay is structured correctly, you know, if it flows. Um, [Denise laughs] uh, these are smart questions.

VINCE: Uhuh.

DENISE: Um, I'd say, like, um, you know, um. Oh, gosh, these are really hard questions. I'd say you have, just, have to have that drive. If it were up to me, anybody who, you know, applied, you know, would get in, because, you know, this is something that they, you know, yearn for. I think as long as you have that desire, as long as you have that passion, and you show it in your writing, I guess? That's a good question.

VINCE: The reason I want you to think about this is because this is the kind of question readers will ask themselves: "What do we want to see in an applicant?" And I'd like to think that those readers will look for writers who are straight to the point, I mean, just the facts, like in journalism. Maybe some story behind it, but really driving the points home. That's just my own bias. So what I'm trying to get you to think about this, is to think about how are you going to structure your essay to move the reader to, to let you into this program. Does that make sense?   The work that it's trying to do is some

DENISE: Uhh—

VINCE: persuasive work. This is the only thing they're going to see about you, next to your transcript, or whatever it is you send along with this application. This is the only thing they're going to see about you, of you.   Um, so this essay, not only is it going

DENISE: Yeah.

VINCE: to address why are you interested in journalism, and what are your career goals, but it's gonna to do some work. And when I say "work," I mean it's like trying to convince an audience that you're it, a qualified applicant. So, with that said, I'm going to ask you this question and see if you can answer now: What are you trying to do, with this paper?

Later in the consultation, Vince refers again to the writer's narrative about being inspired to become a journalist by Christiane Amanpour. "I like the story," he says, "but it's not doing the *work* it should do." "The danger," Vince reiterates, "is that you're not answering the questions fully. First, write down the answers: 'I want to be a journalist because of X, Y, Z.' Then say what your career goals are." Here we see that Vince

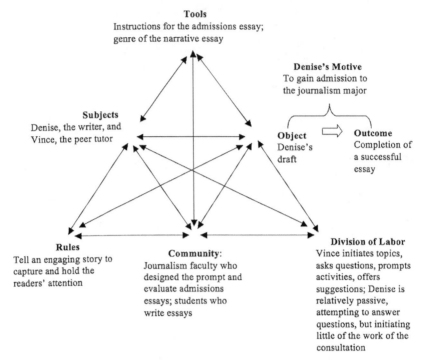

Figure 3.2. Conflicting Activity Systems: Denise's Perspective

has carefully analyzed the rhetorical situation. He's read between the lines of the prompt to understand its implicit purpose. Readers, he reasons, will look to see if the writer has answered the prompt fully. They'll want to be persuaded of the writer's qualifications. While Denise's narrative approach may be effective, Vince has strong doubts. And so he struggles with Denise, trying to convince her that his plan for making an evidence-based argument would be more effective than her approach to telling a story.

USING ACTIVITY THEORY TO EXPLICATE
CONFLICTS IN TUTORING

From an activity-systems perspective, Denise and Vince appear to be working toward the same outcome, Denise's successful application essay. But writer and consultant are working at cross-purposes, with different tools, rules, and motives in mind for accomplishing the same task. Figures 3.2 and 3.3, together, highlight these conflicts.

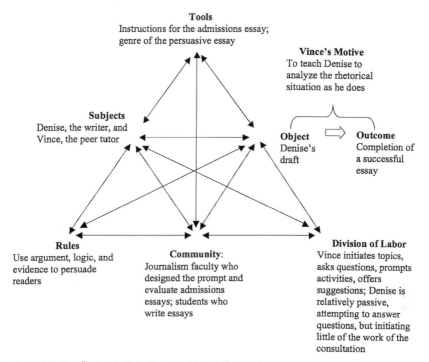

Figure 3.3. Conflicting Activity Systems: Vince's Perspective

One the one hand, Denise has in mind the tool, or genre, of the narrative. By contrast, Vince has in mind the tool, or genre, of the persuasive essay. Neither seems able to imagine an alternative, or some combination of the two. As Heather Trahan (2012) reminds us in her activity theory analysis of a classroom interaction, contradictions like this are central to activity systems. "Contradictions," she points out,

> arise any time diverse individuals interact for the purposes of activity. Their backgrounds, morals, experiences, hopes, talents, and levels of learning will have an effect on the overall composition of the various activities involved. To put it another way, when humans come together in a single activity system to "do" an activity, some of these folks will necessarily interpret and/or carry out the activity in a multitude of assorted, often contradictory ways. (57)

An activity-theory lens through which to examine tutoring focuses our attention on such conflicts: what are their origins and possible consequences? What options can we imagine for addressing, though perhaps not smoothing out or erasing, conflicts? In the case of Denise and Vince, effective tutoring is hampered because Vince seems unable to articulate why his approach might be more effective. It's clear to him, but because Denise doesn't know what he's up to, what his goals are for the consultation, she has difficulty seeing the rhetorical situation as he does. For his part, Vince is knowledgeable about explicating rhetorical situations. He knows what to do. He knows productive questions to ask. And he engages Denise meaningfully in that work. Questions such as "Suppose you were the reader of this application essay; what would you look for?" are promising questions for prompting the writer to explicate the situation.

TROUBLING THE ROLE OF TUTOR "EXPERT"—AGAIN

Now Vince needs a way to step back from what he thinks he knows, to talk with Denise explicitly about why he's working the way he is. But Vince is constrained by his underlying assumptions about teaching. In spite of his writing center training to the contrary, there remains a strong pull for him to slip into lecture mode, where *teaching* is synonymous with *telling*. Throughout the transcript, Victor sounds authoritative, teacherly. His stance, the role he constructs for himself, is a roadblock. Vince talks at Denise, rather than guiding her to tap into and perhaps expand her own conceptions about what might constitute an effective application essay in this situation. He hasn't asked Denise about her interpretation of the rhetorical situation, or her approach to composing a response. He hasn't asked the reasons for the choices she has made. Vince's own transfer of knowledge about explicating rhetorical knowledge, then, is of limited use, because a tutor's task is more complex than just transferring what he knows. Vince needs to use what he knows to help the Denise repurpose what she knows. But in these few minutes, Vince doesn't have strategies at hand for doing that. This is difficult even for the most experienced teachers. Vince's confidence in his own view obscures other possibilities, among them that Denise might revise her narrative about Christiane Amanpour to make it an effective argument about why she wants to major in journalism, and what her career goals are. Where, Vince and Denise might ask together, might the rules and conventions of narrative intersect with those of the persuasive essay?

EXPLICATING THE ACTIVITY SYSTEM OF TUTORING

As this excerpt demonstrates, activity theory sheds light on two distinct activities: the activity of the writing, in this case the activity of composing an application essay, and the activity of the tutoring session itself. While Vince is focused on the work of the essay itself, in terms of the *work* of this writing center consultation, the "division of labor" between Denise and Vince is troubled. Vince is doing all the heavy lifting: topics, questions, activities, and suggestions for revision are all initiated solely by him. As the consultation unfolds, he has more and more to say, the writer less and less. Alternatively, if Denise were invited to describe her approach, and to think about what it affords, what it leaves out, then, with some prompting, she might discover revision options for herself. In short, she might engage in learning-as-problem-solving, not just listening to Vince lecture. In order for this to happen, however, Vince would first have to move from tutoring-as-expert-knowing to tutoring-as-inquiry. He'd have to turn his attention to discovering what Denise understands and what she doesn't yet know.

Vince asks lots of productive questions for figuring out the rhetorical situation. His genre awareness lets him know that Denise's essay must do more than tell an entertaining story. Likewise, my almost daily conversations with Vince about his tutoring taught me what an unusually reflective practitioner he is. Vince thinks carefully about his work, and he tries consciously and deliberately to learn from his experiences in order to improve. At the moment, however, reflection *after* the fact comes more easily to Vince than reflection-in-action. This particular consultation suggests that, whatever prior knowledge tutors bring with them to the writing center, they require additional education and training to make productive use of it, because in a tutoring situation, transferring what the tutor knows is not enough. He has to help the writer transfer, and perhaps trouble, what she knows. First, tutors such as Vince need reinforcement for valued practices in tutoring, such as negotiating an agenda with the writer. In this consultation, Vince's purpose might have been clearer to Denise if he had taken time in the opening minutes of the consultation to talk with her about a plan for working together. They needed to name what work Denise's essay has done, what work it has not yet done, and they needed to set some priorities for both tutoring and revision after the consultation.

Second, tutors need to learn to provide scaffolding to enable writers to make use of the knowledge tutors bring with them. Consultants need to name and explain the cognitive processes they use, or to echo Lerner (2007), "to make visible the thinking and problem-solving processes underlying [a] performance" (62). By inviting writers into their thinking processes, modeling them, and discussing them explicitly, tutors may more effectively engage writers in learning. Finally, alternative models of teaching might be affordances for tutors such as Vince. Instead of teaching-as-telling, Vince might be helped by thinking of his role as tutor in terms of Vygotsky's (1978) "zone of proximal development" (ZPD), which begins, not with deficit, but with what the writer *does* know, what she *can* do independently (86). (See Thompson et al. 2009 and Nordlof 2014 for extended discussions of Vygotsky's ZPD and its applications to writing center tutoring practices.) An activity-theory analysis of the work of this consultation suggests that, instead of lecturing Denise, Victor might more usefully re-imagine his role as more capable peer, with the goal of tapping into the writer's prior knowledge. Understanding the rhetorical situation, then, would include not only explicating the essay prompt, but also learning what the writer brings to the table to interpret that prompt, and what prior writing experiences and processes inform *her* approach.

ASSUMPTIONS UNDERPINNING AN ACTIVITY-SYSTEMS APPROACH TO TUTORING

As the explication of these transcript excerpts illustrate, three key assumptions underpin an activity-systems approach to writing center work. First, within an activity system, writing develops collaboratively in relations with others. It is not the work of the solitary individual, but a social activity. Tutors do not bank their disciplinary expertise into the empty heads of tutees. Rather, through conversation tutors assist writers to develop their own understanding of specific contexts and purposes for writing. Through dialogue tutors learn what writers know and what "tools" and alternative "subjects," such as the teacher, may provide further information in order to write effectively in a particular situation. Instead of assuming the role of specialist, peer consultants may collaborate with writers to develop a list of questions to investigate further, about the related course content, for example, about the content and form of the required writing task, about the style of documentation, and so forth.

Second, activity theory teaches tutors that writing is bound by a particular context. To this end, Nancy Grimm (1999), in *Good Intentions: Writing Center Work for Postmodern Times*, frames tutoring in terms of contemporary understandings of literacy theory. Like Russell (1995) and other activity theorists, Grimm sees writing not as an "autonomous" skill, existing apart from context, but, instead, as Brian Street and other literacy specialists have urged, as "ideological," implicated in power relations. "Literacy," according the ideological view, is not a set of skills that writers either have or lack, and which they come to the writing center to get. Rather, *literacy* includes an array of reading and writing practices. Students who visit the writing center bring with them a wide range of multiple literacies. According to this view, writing is not a neutral set of transferable skills, which, once they learn them, writers may take with them, like items in a briefcase, to whatever writing task they face. Instead, students who seek help from the writing center must learn particular kinds of literacies for specific purposes. In short, activity theory offers a framework for understanding what "context-bound" means for literacy instruction, by specifying that contexts for writing include, at a minimum, subjects, objects or motives, tools, outcomes, rules, community, and division of effort. In this way, activity theory offers tutors a way to think about what writing is and how it gets accomplished by naming and bringing to the fore its constitutive aspects.

Third, by situating genre as a tool within a larger activity system, activity theory underscores the importance of genre knowledge in writing center work. As subjects joining with writers to help them accomplish some writing task, tutors must first learn what the object or motive for writing is and then talk with writers about what tools—or genres—may be most appropriate to the task, and what characteristic features and moves those genres entail. In Kristin Walker's (1998) words, "By applying genre theory, tutors can move away from the oppositional poles of generalist and specialist and toward a more unified goal of addressing all clients' specific writing needs" (28).

As the analysis of the excerpts in this chapter demonstrate, activity theory is a useful heuristic for analyzing the work of a tutoring session. As Engeström and Miettinen (1999) explain:

> Activity theory as a unit of analysis calls for complimentarity of the system view and the subject's view. The analyst constructs the activity system as if looking at it from above. At the same time, the analyst must select a subject, a member (or better yet, multiple different members) of the local activity, through whose eyes and interpretations the activity is constructed. This dialectic between the systemic and subjective-partisan views brings the researcher into a dialogical relationship with the local activity under investigation. (10)

In this way, applying the concepts of activity theory, writing center tutors become analysts who examine from the perspectives of both outsider and subject in the activity system of a tutoring session in which they themselves are participants. Transcription analysis can help tutors develop this perspective of participant-researcher.

EXPLICATING ANOTHER CONFLICT: FORM FOLLOWS
FUNCTION—OR DOES IT?

To illustrate further what such analysis might look like, below are excerpts from another consultation. In this session, Tyler, a finance major, brings with him a partial draft of a business letter for a management course. Lena, an English major, is unfamiliar with the communicative landscape of business writing in Management 129, and this assignment in particular: to compose what is referred to as a "bad news letter," in this case, from a manufacturer of a device for swimming in place to a potential retailer. The purpose of the letter, to communicate information, gets lost, because both writer and tutor become preoccupied with the form, rather than the function, of the letter. As Tyler replies, in some frustration, when Lena suggests that the letter must have a *purpose*: "Yeah, but that's not the point. The point of the thing is that you, see, I, the letter refers to, right? But the point isn't, that isn't the point. The point is that, that, that you have the paragraph, so that whatever you use, 'distribution,' 'manufacturing,' whatever, the problem is, you use the paragraphs properly and present the information properly." For Tyler, "proper" presentation takes precedence over meaning; form trumps function.

Transcript Excerpt 4—Tyler and Lena

TYLER: So, so today I could get started where I, as much as I have done.

LENA: Right

TYLER: I have a good start on two paragraphs. I'm supposed to do two more. Of course, they're just specific content paragraphs. Are you familiar with Management 129?

LENA: No, I am not,   but it looks like it's a very specific format.

TYLER: Okay.

TYLER: Yes, it is.   Right, so, and so each paragraph does, the content

LENA: Okay.

TYLER: of it has to be, you know, specified. But anyway,

LENA: So do you think you have that down?

TYLER: but I know that, I know that part of it, I, you know, it's the, it's the it, the writing part maybe, that um, I mean, as far as, as far as, I mean, I, I've al—, I've been a fairly decent writer. I've had another career and another life [Tyler laughs], but, um, and my punctuation is fairly decent, and my spelling I've always been conscious of that. Sentence structure, uh, probably needs some work. Sometimes they get lengthy,   but I'm really

LENA: Yeah.

TYLER: concentrating on breaking those down. As long as I don't break them down too much. I don't want to be eeee-eeee-eeee, right?   I don't

LENA: Yeah.

TYLER: want to go too far with it. Er, and, and this business stuff is supposed to be written from the you, a you attitude.

LENA: Oh, like second person?

TYLER: Yes. You want to, you want to concentrate on your reader, you want them to be the focus, not yourself.   Yeah, so—(4 sec.)

LENA: Okay.   So what would you like to start with?

As this excerpt illustrates, from the start, Tyler and Lena talk at crosspurposes. One learning goal for the bad news letter is for students to demonstrate their ability to apply the business-writing concept of the "you attitude," which, as Tyler attempts to explain, is reader-centered prose that avoids "I" and "we" to draw attention not to the writer but to what the reader has to gain from the communication. But Lena, unfamiliar with this principle, mistakenly assumes that the "you" Tyler refers to here is the same "you" she's been warned against in writing literary criticism, the second-person "you."

As this session continues, Tyler explains that he's drafted the first two paragraphs of the four-paragraph letter, and then he and Lena agree to generate ideas for the remaining two:

Transcript Excerpt 5—Tyler and Lena

LENA: How about, um, why don't we start off and I'll write down some of the ideas that you tell me. And I'll just ask you a couple questions about the third paragraph. That way we can get some ideas down on paper. And then we can go from there. (2 sec.) So, for the third paragraph, what is it supposed to be?

TYLER: It's the bad news. This is a bad news, um, response. It's a bad news response to a, um, to a request from a potential retail seller.

LENA: What is the bad news that—

TYLER: The bad news is that um, uh, the manufacturer isn't yet prepared to ship internationally.

LENA: Okay. And this is what you're supposed to be telling?

TYLER: Mm-hmm, but you're supposed to do it, you're supposed to *subordinate* it. (3 sec.)

LENA: Subordinate?

TYLER: Yeah, subordinate it into a [inaudible] sentence.

LENA: Okay. (4 sec.) Are you, is there a certain format for telling,   or are

TYLER: Yes.

LENA: you supposed to—

TYLER: Well the format is, the format is, it's supposed to be in
this third paragraph, and it's supposed to be subordinated. In other words,
in the end of a complex sentence or—   Okay? (2 sec.)

LENA: Oh, so it's, okay—
Do you, is it, any specific form, like cause or, cause and effect, due to
this? We aren't able to do this? Or

TYLER: Well, see, I, I, I started, I started
preparing—

LENA: like are the first two paragraphs setting   it up?

TYLER: Yes.   Yes, exactly.

LENA: Yeah. So let's see—

TYLER: And this is it right here. My first one is a bit, is
a bummer.   And then the reasons. (5 sec.)

LENA: Okay.   And then the third
paragraph is bad news. [Reading from the assignment sheet] "State
the bad news clearly and concisely. Emphasize any good news.
De-emphasize bad news." (4 sec.) and you're supposed to do it indirect. (2 sec.) So let's see, the "buffer" is, you've got to "begin with
a neutral or positive statement." [Reading from Tyler's draft] "Your
interest in swim cards is exciting." That's, "Swim cards were developed
to satisfy a desire to swim laps in a small pool. Swimming is a non-
impact sport that provides excellent aerobic exercise. Avid swimmers
are buying"   "the swim cards in growing numbers."

TYLER: Mm-hmm.

TYLER: Cords. Cords. Swim *cords*.

LENA: *Cords*, okay, consistency, C-O-R-D-S.

Again, because she is unfamiliar with the disciplinary rules and conventions of business writing, Lena struggles to understand Tyler's context for writing. At the same time, Lena is working hard to figure out the
form and to be helpful.

Transcript Excerpt 6—Tyler and Lena

TYLER: See, I'm right here (2 sec), but I don't know any good news.

LENA: I think the good news is that the retailer can get the product, but
not until July.

TYLER: Yeah, right.

LENA: So I think you need to have a sentence here, "We can't at the present moment send you the cords. But, based on the pace of growth, we will be able to do it in July." So it's saying the bad thing, we can't give it to you right now, but—

TYLER: But, you know, but you know, you can't use that. You can't use "can't." You can't use "we" (2 sec).

LENA: Oh, okay [Lena laughs]. Man, this is tough.

TYLER: Yeah, okay, yeah, it becomes a word game doesn't it?

LENA: Yeah, so saying it, but there's something in there, something about "this is not available," or "it's not ready for ship—." Can you use the word "not" at all?

TYLER: Unh-uh.   Can't use "not." Can't use anything negative. Can't use

LENA: Hummm.

TYLER: "hope," "trust," "if," um—[returns to consult the assignment instructions]: "Don't use any negative words."

Tyler, it seems, is stumped about how to develop the fourth and final paragraph of the letter, which, according to his professor's instructions, must end on a positive note. "See, I'm right here," Tyler says, "but I don't know any good news." Although Lena does not understand the genre of the bad news letter, she nevertheless tells Tyler how he should write the paragraph. In doing so, Lena turns her attention to the text, rather than to helping Tyler understand the activity of writing the business letter. With her directive, "So I think you need to have a sentence here," she begins to compose the paragraph for the writer, with overconfidence that leads them further astray. Because, like the writer, the consultant is excessively concerned with the formal features of the letter, and because she does not understand those features, the session reaches an impasse. In this exchange, like the one above with Wacey and Eric, the tutor's strategy is characterized by a quest for answers, for prescriptions to fix what ails the letter. Lena is in search of an expert's role, a space from which she can speak definitively about both the assignment and what she thinks should be Tyler's priorities for revision.

One hundred lines later in the transcript, the impasse begins to break after Lena urges Tyler to return again to his assignment instructions and re-read more carefully the imaginary scenario upon which the letter is based:

Transcript Excerpt 7—Tyler and Lena

LENA: Say, in the future will the cords be available internationally? (4 sec.) You also talk about "distribution." Small, right? Or is it growing?

TYLER: It's supposed to be, you know, it has to be four paragraphs
because you have to

LENA: Four paragraphs.

TYLER: have the "buffer," the "reason," the "bad news," and the "positive."
"Sixteen to twenty sentences altogether," but (2 sec.) develop, however I word it as, as, well, and, um, so, and I, and I do, I do have some
material I can add in here.

LENA: Yeah, to give it that length that it needs?

TYLER: Yeah (2 sec). Um (2 sec.).

LENA: It's just these down here are getting kind of skimpy (4 sec.). Let's
read the scenario again, to see if there's any useful information you
could add. [Tyler and Lena read silently together.] (12 sec.)

TYLER: Yeah, this one, this one. I know I can do something with because
they tell you that you can, uh, send her a free sample. You know, so
you know, that's some material for words.   Right?

LENA: Okay.   Yeah, and
that could, yeah, or you could put that into the fourth paragraph,
where you can't send it until July, but "we're happy to send you a free
sample to see how you like our product now." That could be the good
news, emphasizing the good news.

TYLER: Oh, you know, you're right.   That's right.

LENA: Yeah.

Tyler begins by repeating the required outline of the letter: "buffer,"
"reason," "bad news," and "positive ending." Even as Lena, too, remains
hyper-concerned with the length requirement, his questions at the
beginning of this excerpt, along with their collaborative talk, trouble
their preoccupation with form, leading Tyler to an "aha moment" about
function, in which he comes to realize that, while form is important, he
does, indeed, have meaningful information to convey to his would-be
business client.

MAKING ROOM FOR MISCONCEPTIONS—AGAIN

Tyler's initial misconception about writing is the key to helping him
move forward as a learner—again, not by identifying and then robbing
him of it, but by allowing him to hold his misconception as valid while
simultaneously inviting him to explore another, competing possibility.
Here the tutor does not tell the writer what to write, or ignore, even
temporarily, the formal features of the letter. Rather, she confirms the
student's own discovery that there is, in fact, good news supplied in the
scenario, which may fit, appropriately, as part of the required positive

ending. This provides Tyler with an opportunity to pit two concepts against each other: the first, that business writing is a meaningless "word game"; the second, that one may communicate meaning effectively, even within a narrowly prescribed form. This second concept destabilizes the first concept enough for the student to realize something new about the assignment: that form more usefully follows function. Tyler's initial misconception, that the purpose of the business letter is to "present the information properly," can be weighed against a new, more complicated possibility, that he first needed to understand the communicative situation, in order to make meaning in a genre recognizable to an expert in his discipline. Importantly, Lena prompts Tyler by reframing the activity of the consultation, from a fixing-the-draft task to the activity of close reading. Figures 3.4 and 3.5 again highlight the conflicting perspectives regarding the activities of the consultation.

From her perspective, Lena seems to recognize that an implicit learning goal of Tyler's assignment is to demonstrate his ability to carefully analyze the business scenario on which the letter is based. As an English major, Lena is familiar with turning to the text for answers. She understands that writing an effective response depends, first, on carefully explicating the text. Together, Tyler and Lena begin to construct an alternative position available to the writer but previously unseen, the position of making meaning as a business communicator.

"EMERGENT EXPERTISE" IN TUTORING

While conflicting objectives initially appear to be a roadblock to teaching and learning in this consultation, as Clay Spinuzzi (2008) points out, contradictions are the heart of the matter in activity systems (122). Contradictions are ever-present in human activities. In Trahan's (2012) words, "[C]ontradictions do not indicate failure—they indicate life. Let us not be discouraged by these," she offers, "but rather take them as motivating facts" (67). Engaging with tutors to examine consultation transcripts like these through the lens of activity theory can prompt tutors to identify such conflicts and to consider varied alternatives for addressing them. What's more, an activity-theory approach to tutoring can guide peer consultants to reconsider their roles, particularly in light of the ongoing conversation in writing center studies regarding "expertise." To return to the literature on expert and novice practices in problem solving from the field of science, in "Lab Technicians and High School Student Interns—Who Is Scaffolding Whom?: On Forms of Emergent Expertise," Pei-Ling Hsu and Wolff-Michael Roth find that

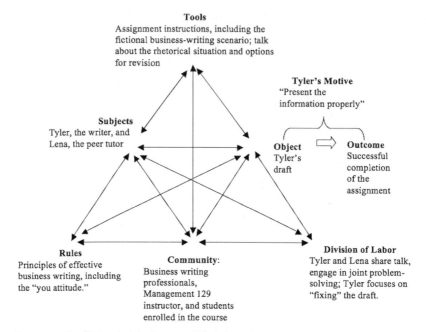

Figure 3.4. Conflicting Activity Systems: Tyler's Perspective

scaffolding newcomers into a community of practice is not a one-way process where the expert or more capable peer supports the development of the novice (Hsu and Roth 2008). Rather, because learning is social and dialogical, knowlegeability is a two-way street. In their study of high school students from a Canadian public school, who were invited to work with scientists/technicians in a neighboring university biology lab, Hsu and Roth became interested in the transactional processes by which students came to participate in scientific practice. Based on their observations of newcomers becoming enculturated into this community of practice, they propose the notion of "emergent expertise" to describe that participation, where "expertise is not constituted in individuals but emergent during participant's transactions with available resources" (22). In other words, perhaps expertise is not located *in* individuals, either in the tutor or the in tutee, for example, in a writing center consultation; rather expertise emerges through their interactions. Rather than ask who has expertise, then, or who is a specialist, with an activity-theory perspective we can look more closely at the activity system of writing center consultations, asking what tutors and tutees are *doing* together—what *activities* they're engaging in, and how those activities either forward or inhibit learning: what are their goals and intentions,

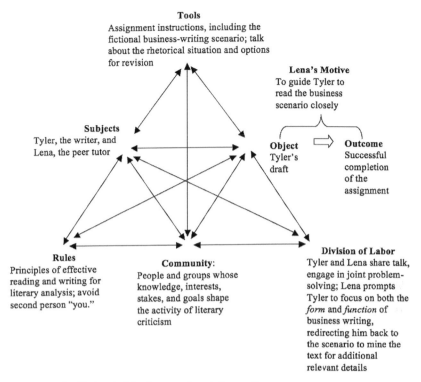

Tools
Assignment instructions, including the fictional business-writing scenario; talk about the rhetorical situation and options for revision

Lena's Motive
To guide Tyler to read the business scenario closely

Subjects
Tyler, the writer, and Lena, the peer tutor

Object
Tyler's draft

Outcome
Successful completion of the assignment

Rules
Principles of effective reading and writing for literary analysis; avoid second person "you."

Community:
People and groups whose knowledge, interests, stakes, and goals shape the activity of literary criticism

Division of Labor
Tyler and Lena share talk, engage in joint problem-solving; Lena prompts Tyler to focus on both the *form* and *function* of business writing, redirecting him back to the scenario to mine the text for additional relevant details

Figure 3.5. Conflicting Activity Systems: Lena's Perspective

what objects or products result from their activities, what tools are used, what rules and conventions circumscribe their activities, what are the larger communities in which these activities occur, and how is effort divided in a consultation?

This chapter ends with an inquiry into tutoring via an activity theory analysis of transcript excerpts. Key to this assignment is its collaborative design. One goal is to enact the collaborative principle of inquiry-based learning. Another is to further challenge the "expert-novice" distinction explored in this chapter, which mistakenly assumes that the expert knows and distributes formal knowledge, while the novice learns by taking up and imitating the strategies doled out by the more competent expert. In contrast, this assignment assumes that novice and experienced tutors work together to make new knowledge by analyzing data gleaned from transcripts of tutoring. Finally, unlike so many "group" assignments in school, which students divide up into separate parts to complete individually, this assignment is intended to avoid that pitfall explicitly. Instead, this assignment invites writing consultants to be of two minds simultaneously: to work together to analyze a transcript, while, at the same time, studying the group's workings as an activity system whose purpose is to learn about tutoring by engaging in this activity theory analysis.

ASSIGNMENT: COLLABORATIVE ACTIVITY
THEORY TRANSCRIPT ANALYSIS

Using activity theory as a conceptual framework for analysis, write a collaborative essay with a small group of classmates, analyzing a transcript of a single tutoring session, selected from the group.

Your essay should briefly describe the consultation you choose to write about. It should accurately explain activity theory and demonstrate its use as a framework for thinking about writing and tutoring.

Your essay should also include a reflection on what you have learned as a result of completing this assignment together with your group. Do not divide up the paper into separate sections for each group member to complete independently. Instead, each person should contribute equally to writing all parts of the essay. The purpose is to work together in a collaborative activity system, even as you use activity theory to examine not only a tutoring consultation but also, in reflection, your own group's operation as an activity system.

To Do:

- Record at least one tutoring session in anticipation of this assignment. You must obtain written permission from the writer before you record. You must turn in a completed consent form, including both the tutee's signature and yours.

- Student identity *must* be protected: do not use the writer's real name, and do not include identifying details about the student.

- After you have successfully recorded a tutoring session you would like to write about, listen to the recording several times. Using Gilewicz and Thonus's "Close Vertical Transcription" as a model, transcribe at least fifteen minutes of the consultation.

- Share and discuss your transcript with your group. Select one from the group to use as the basis for this assignment.

- Using the analysis in this chapter as a model, write a paper analyzing your consultation, through the lens of activity theory. Approach this paper with an open mind; feel free to focus on positive aspects of your consultation as well as problematic elements.

- If this assignment works well, then you will demonstrate that you understand and can apply activity theory to your analysis. In this effort, you will be engaged in a process of *discovery*: ask what the tutor and tutees are *doing* together—what *activities* they're engaged in, and how those activities either forward or inhibit learning: what are their goals and intentions, what objects or products result from their activities, what tools are used, what rules and conventions circumscribe their activities, what are the larger communities in which these activities occur, and how is effort divided in the tutorial? Finally, what has your group learned by examining your transcript and your work together?

Your Essay Should Include the Following:

- An introduction, including a brief description of the session and your specific focus for analysis.
- An analysis of the consultation, using activity theory as a conceptual framework.
- Several substantial excerpts from the transcript as evidence.
- Concluding reflections that explain what your group has thought about and learned as a result of working together in your own activity system on this assignment.

Attach a transcript with your paper. You must also turn in your recording and a signed consent form.

4

COMMONPLACE RHETORICAL MOVES OF SESSION NOTES

Participating in a genre means not just producing a text that looks like the ones that are usually produced in that milieu but having purposes, for action and, therefore, communication, that are recognized and allowed for within that context and for which the genre has emerged adaptively as the appropriate vehicle.

–Patrick Dias, Aviva Freedman, Peter Medway, Anthony Paré (1999), *Worlds Apart: Acting and Writing in Academic and Workplace Contexts.*

IN THIS CHAPTER

- **Focal Documents:** sample session notes
- **Purpose:** to document the work of tutoring sessions for writers, faculty, and writing center staff
- **Conceptual Framework for Analysis:** discourse analysis
- **Data:** corpus of seven hundred notes
- **Assignment:** "Coding Samples of Your Session Notes"

As I noted in the introduction, when I use the word *theory*, I mean to evoke its multiple meanings and functions, among them that theory is a *heuristic*, a tool of discovery and invention. The previous chapter explored some of the ways activity theory can be used as such a tool to discover not only the context for writing, but also the workings of a tutorial as an activity system. This chapter brings to the fore another conceptual framework, or heuristic, discourse analysis. Like activity theory, discourse analysis is a useful tool for studying writing center work, in particular, our language-using practices. Researchers such as Laurel Black (1998) in *Between Talk and Teaching: Reconsidering the Writing Conference*, and Magdalena Gilewicz and Terese Thonus in "Close Vertical Transcription in Writing Center Training and Research" provide excellent models for doing conversation analysis (Gilewicz and Thonus 2003). Discourse analysis may also be used to examine documents. This chapter uses discourse analysis to examine the document of session

DOI: 10.7330/9781607325826.c004

reports, reaching back to chapter 2 to explore some of the ways valued practices for tutoring are reflected in these notes.

DISCOVERING THE GENRE OF SESSION NOTES

As early as our initial day-long orientation for novice tutors, newcomers in our writing center are introduced to the practice of composing written follow-ups, conference summaries, tutor reports, or what we call "session notes," after each consultation. Such reports are commonplace in writing centers, made more so by the ubiquity of online management software, such as TutorTrac and WCOnline, which archive notes and allow them to be sent to recipients electronically. Tutors usually compose reports after each consultation, in the ten to fifteen minutes between sessions, and then email them to writers. Tutor reports serve a variety of purposes for multiple, sometimes conflicting, audiences. In our case, session notes vary widely in content, but typically detail the work of the consultation, direct writers to additional resources they can access independently, beyond the consultation, and make suggestions for next steps to take in revision. Writers may share these notes with professors, who sometimes request evidence of work in the writing center, as part of an assignment or for extra credit. In addition to writers and teachers, to prepare for a consultation with a student who has visited the writing center previously, tutors often review the archive of notes before a session to learn what the writer has worked on in past sessions and what recurring concerns should be addressed in a follow-up. Administrators, too, can track the work of consultations via tutor reports.

Novice peer tutors have lots of questions about how to compose this unfamiliar genre: when should session notes be written? What is their purpose? Who is the audience? What do readers do with conference summaries? What kinds of information should be included? What should be left out? How much detail is expected? What should be the tone? Simply telling new tutors isn't very effective. Instead, we invite tutors to begin by studying several examples of session notes to unearth commonplace norms that characterize notes produced in our writing center. Our aim is to guide tutors to *discover* for themselves the characteristics or features of conference summaries. Then, as they begin tutoring, consultants gain opportunities to generate or *practice* the strategies needed to produce those characteristics. Drawing on the principles of inquiry-based learning, George Hillocks (1995) calls such guided discovery and practice "gateway activities," or "strategies of inquiry and ways of generating discourse features" (149). Such activities, he explains, "engage students in using difficult production strategies with varying levels of support and lead eventually to independence" (150). This gateway activity is based on the assumption that telling students how to write session notes—even modeling for them—isn't sufficient for learning. Learning to compose this genre requires that tutors discover for themselves the discourse features of tutor reports and then practice producing those features repeatedly over time, with periodic feedback. To that end, working from several examples, which are typical of notes composed in our writing center, newcomers collaborate during orientation to develop an agreed upon list of characteristics of effective session notes. Then, in follow-up meetings, once tutors have drafted some authentic conference summaries of their own, we compare them to the list of discourse features identified previously. In the process, consultants question and amend their initial list, based on evolving values and collective understandings of the rhetorical work of tutor reports.

The rhetorical work of session notes is the focus of this chapter. To begin, with the above gateway activity in mind, examine the following examples of this everyday document of writing center work. I selected these samples for teaching purposes, because they are typical of session notes from our writing center. While session notes are sometimes shorter or longer, these four notes all include a moderate level of detail. As a group, they exhibit some of the commonplace moves we find among session notes in our writing center. Along with typical moves, this document set also illustrates variations, including both strengths and weaknesses. On the balance, however, as a tool for coaching newcomers to learn to write session notes, I selected these examples because they demonstrate multiple traits I regard as effective, which I hope novices will notice and emulate. With this goal in mind, I've not included examples of notes I regard as ineffective.

For now, give them a cursory read, looking for recurrent patterns, repeated moves or themes of significance. Later, you can compare your list of commonplace moves to those that emerged from a study of seven hundred tutor reports. For example, you'll notice that all four notes below summarize the work of the tutorial, sometimes explicitly, as with the phrase "Here is brief summary of our consultation" in Note 2, sometimes implicitly, as in Note 1. Summary of the work done, then, is a repeated rhetorical pattern found in most of the conference summaries produced in our writing center. Now see what other recurring rhetorical moves you can find:

Session Note 1:

Tonight, we looked at your next history paper assignment. Most of what we discussed was trying to make sense of all the questions your professor has given you; you have the notes for these on your assignment sheet, but as a reminder, here are some key points to think about in writing your paper:

Thesis that can address an overarching question! We came up with the question of "how did changes in the global and local conditions of the war during the New England, Mid-Atlantic, and Southern Phases impact the American Revolution?" Check with your professor to make sure this is an approach that will appropriately provide for all of the smaller questions she wants you to address.

Find a way to integrate all those smaller questions as subpoints to a larger argument that answers a question.

We discussed organizing your discussion as a progression through the phases, New England to Mid-Atlantic to Southern, emphasizing the links between them and how they impacted and/or drew on each other.

Outline to get your ideas out!

Best of luck with your paper, and thank you for visiting the Writing Center!

Session Note 2:

Hello Walley,

Thanks for coming into the UWC today. Here is brief summary of our consultation. You brought in your memoirs about your time in the ROTC from 1968 to 1972. Your two main concerns were that you wanted your memoirs to sound as if we were sitting down at a bar and you were telling me a story. Furthermore, you wanted your memoirs to be free of any grammatical errors before being published.

Overall, your memoirs sound great! The story captivated me and I would love to finish reading it when you have finished the final chapter.

However, we did observe that there were some issues with comma placement. We went over some sentences that needed commas and you were able to identify where the commas should go with little of my assistance. I gave you a great handout about commas that I recommend you utilize when you continue editing the memoirs.

Additionally, when you see places where you use parentheses, consider whether or not they are necessary and if they can be eliminated. I think it will make your story sound more fluent.

Lastly, look over the notes that we took on the two copies of the draft. Cannot wait to read the finished copy! Que te vaya bien mi amigo y que tengas un buen viaje.

Sinceramente,

J.R.

Session Note 3:

Hello, Sarah!

Today we looked over your application for the HIM scholarship. We tried to cut for content as we went, but I was a bit hesitant to cut for wordiness, not knowing the conventions of this scientific genre. Definitely ask your professor to help with this when you submit it to her for review. Also ask her about how to respond to the last question.

We decided your best course of action would be to write out answers for both possible interpretations—the personal theory you are working with as a researcher, or a preexisting larger theory of which your research will investigate one nuanced part—and present both to your professor for her advice. She probably knows best what this application requires, so definitely trust her advice on this.

Also, once you've finished your draft, pay attention to introductory commas in your revisions. Use the handout I gave you to help you with this if you need help.

Best of luck finishing your application, and thank you for visiting the Writing Center!

Session Note 4:

Hey Victoria, thanks for coming to the University Writing Center! Here's a brief summary of what we discussed today, I hope it helps:

Longman Dictionary: Some of the word choices that you have made do not necessarily relate to the message you are trying to explain. This can be caused by several reasons; I want to focus on how you can get a better understanding of these words. By using *Longman Dictionary*, words not only simplified but explained when the use of the word would be proper. Here is the website: http://www.ldoceonline.com/.

Articles: We discussed how you were missing some articles. The omission of these articles can, and will, have an effect on how a reader understands your message. The worksheet I have given you is designed to clarify various misunderstanding.

Readability/Grammar: Your understanding of the English language is very strong, more so than my own! I want to congratulate you for that accomplishment. The words has/have/ had obviously gave you an issue when writing them. Pay attention to how you are using these words.

Overall, I felt that the reflection piece was very strong. Although we weren't able to start reading the actual annotated bib. due to time constraints, I hope that what we did touch on can help you better revise your overall paper.

Best Wishes,

V.

MAKING THE EVERYDAY DOCUMENT OF SESSION NOTES AN OBJECT OF INQUIRY

I begin this chapter with a description of this simple gateway activity and a few accompanying session notes to illustrate a larger point, which motivates each chapter in this book: the everyday documents of writing center work, such as session notes, and the activities they mediate, like the rudimentary genre analysis we engage in with novice tutors, invite further systematic research. But the very ubiquity and mundanity of commonplace documents can cause us to miss opportunities to look more closely at and around the texts of writing center work. This may explain why, to date, there is so little research about tutor reports. This chapter details what we learned in our writing center when we took up session notes as an object of inquiry. We began with the simple exigency that opens this chapter, the need to teach new tutors how to write effective conference summaries. When we meet together with inexperienced tutors at the beginning of a new term, we all feel some anxiety. There is a lot to learn, and quickly. In only a few days, novices will begin consulting, and central to effective tutoring are meaningful session notes composed afterward. Tutors, understandably, are eager to learn how to write good session notes. This need and the activity described above prompted several inquiry questions: "What work do session notes do? What are the commonplace rhetorical moves tutors make in composing session notes? To what ends?" If I could learn the commonplace rhetorical moves of tutor reports, I reasoned, then I could consider, together with tutors, if these are the moves peer consultants *should* make in the first place. If so, I could teach tutors to write effective notes by naming and making these moves explicit. If not, I could collaborate with tutors to identify alternative moves our writing center values, and then teach those rhetorical features instead. These initial questions speak to the *production* of session notes. That's the focus of this chapter, which is the first phase of a larger study of session notes.

The second phase of research, which is ongoing and beyond the scope of this chapter, concerns the *reception* of session notes, asking, "What do writers do with session notes? Do notes inform revision? If so, in what ways? What other purposes do session notes serve for writers?" The questions that drive this second phase of research are perhaps the more consequential. After all, if writers don't find session notes useful, if conference summaries don't spur revision and the writer's development, then their rhetorical features don't much matter in the first place. But first we need thick description of the work of session notes. Importantly, the account that follows is less about findings and more about the generative thinking that resulted, for both tutors and administrators, when we began to examine tutor reports closely. Turning an everyday exigency into a research project like this one not only illuminates what, exactly, is happening in our writing center, but it also invites change in practices, along with further inquiry.

FRAMING THE PROBLEM: AUDIENCE AND ACCESS

The existing scholarly conversation about tutor reports is limited, focused less on the *work* that session notes do and more on persistent anxieties about audience and access. Michael Pemberton's (1995) "Writing Center Ethics: Sharer's and Seclusionists," the first published article that I'm aware of on this subject, maps the pros and cons of two contrary positions concerning the audience of conference summaries. While the audience for tutor reports is an important consideration, a quick tour of the literature reveals how Pemberton's initial framing has taken hold and worked to narrow and dominate the conversation about session notes to little else. The "sharers," explains Pemberton, advocate sharing tutor reports with faculty to aid in tracking and supporting student progress and development. One potential downside of this stance is that it may undermine student relationships with the writing center. The "seclusionists," on the other hand, discourage sharing information with faculty via tutor reports, privileging, instead, the protection of student privacy. This position, however, may unintentionally support the misperception that visiting the writing center is something shameful, which ought to be kept secret, even from a teacher. Pemberton offers a compromise: share session notes with faculty only with written student permission beforehand (14).

Echoing Pemberton's concern about faculty access, Anneke J. Larrance and Barbara Brady open with several questions:

How and why do writing centers write reports or narratives following a tutorial? To whom is the report addressed? How is the information used that is contained in the report? Is there a relationship between the size of the college or the number of writing center visits and the decision to provide a follow-up report? What does the written report look like? (Larrance and Brady 1995, 5)

Acknowledging that the *form* of tutor reports varies widely, like Pemberton, Larrance and Brady give little attention to the *content*—the rhetorical work—of session notes. Rather, they are interested in what they term "patterns of use and rationale of written writing center conference follow-up." They report that "the majority of writing centers communicate with faculty outside the centers only with student consent, as 85% of students working in writing centers can maintain their privacy" (7). They conclude, "Our original debate about the audience of written follow-ups is over. We are convinced that faculty AND students should be included as readers" (7).

Parting company with Pemberton and Larrance and Brady, Kim Jackson (1996) advocates keeping written follow-up reports in house. In her view, session notes are not intended for faculty *or* students but for writing center staff, as she puts it, "for our own educational purposes, which includes educating ourselves about what we do and why" (13). Attempting to extend the conversation about tutor reports to address "the purposes of session notes and what information we should include," Jackson finds her efforts stymied by her own writing center staff's hyper-concern, again, with questions of audience and access. Tutors object to sharing session notes with faculty because they recognize, rightly, that any session report is limited, an incomplete account of a consultation. Even more problematic, Jackson's account includes the description of an instance in which a faculty member unfairly judges a tutor's ability because of a grammatical error in a conference summary (12).

Amplifying the collective writing center narrative about tutor reports and the audience anxiety they generate, Glenda Conway (1998) frames the problem this way: "When writing center personnel routinely send tutoring session reports to the teachers of their clients, they have no way of knowing what use, if any, teachers will make of the information that's conveyed" (9). Her solution is a form completed by writers themselves "on which students may write about their center visit in any way they choose." This puts the onus, not with writing center staff, but with writers themselves to take the initiative to report back to teachers. To shield tutors from "teachers' expectations or concerns," the same form invites teachers to take up concerns about the nature of writing center work with the director herself (12).

REFRAMING THE PROBLEM

As I argued in chapter 2 about the long-standing scholarly conversation concerning anxiety over observations of tutoring, our too-narrow framing of the problem is part of the problem itself, causing attention-blindness to a host of other equally important aspects of session notes, beyond questions of audience and access, which cry out for further research. To that end, Jane Cogie (1998) enlivens the conversation by analyzing data gathered from three surveys regarding perceptions of tutor reports: one of faculty, one of tutors, and another of writers. All three groups viewed session notes shared with teachers positively. With excerpts from multiple examples, Cogie gives significant attention not only to the problem of audience but also to the *content* of session notes. "[T]he conference summary," she concludes, "at least as employed at my institution, is a difficult but, on the balance, worthwhile form" (60). In particular, Cogie's data prompts her to laud "the potential of this form to reinforce the value of their collaborative process for writing center students and tutors, and to extend the benefits of that process to the teacher" (61). Cogie's data, she asserts, "should call into question rejecting summaries merely out of a desire to quash the 'service' or 'handmaiden' stereotype of the writing center" (61).

In another fresh approach to tutor reports, Margaret Weaver (2001) points out that if one aim of writing centers is to engender authority in student writers, then they can't be merely passive recipients of session notes. Instead, writers must become active makers of knowledge not only within the tutorial but also in the written account that follows. Weaver argues, "we should encourage students and tutors to create jointly told tales" by composing conference summaries together (51). While I am convinced of Weaver's argument, having tried repeatedly to persuade tutors to engage together with tutees to collaborate on session notes, I've had few takers. In my experience, both tutors and writers resist taking time during consultations to compose notes. No matter how valuable this collaborative approach may be, both parties tend to view it as an intrusion, as a time-consuming distraction that takes attention away from the business of tutoring. Although it may be argued that making plans for what the writer will do *after* the consultation *is* the very heart of tutoring, the perception persists that composing session notes is a task to be completed only *after* the tutorial, not during it. Nevertheless, Weaver's concerns about who produces session notes and who has access to them still don't tell us anything about their *content*.

Danielle Cardaro (2014) replicates Cogie's earlier survey research, asking what students and faculty do with the information in session reports.

At the same time, Cardaro follows Weaver's advice about involving writers themselves in their composition. As for the content, Cardaro explains that in her writing center "reports consist of two open-ended questions: 1) What did the client accomplish during the session? and 2) What is the client's revision plan? Clients and consultants decide what details to include in the report together" (2). Her results show that students use conference summaries to recall the work of the tutorial and to remind themselves of revision plans. In keeping with Cogie's earlier findings, Cardaro confirms that faculty, too, make positive use of session notes. Cardaro encourages faculty to use session notes in a variety of innovative ways to support vertical writing instruction in a newly designed general education curriculum.

Another recent study, Rita Malenczyk's (2013), investigates what she terms "the community-building function" of session notes (75). Examining tutor reports through the lens of organizational rhetoric, Malenczyk argues that these documents "are not just exchanges between the tutor and one or more people but are, rather, part of an institutional network of relationships, given that a writing center is typically part of a larger educational context, be it . . . a school, college, or university" (77). In a first pass, Malenczyk notes that nearly all of the 143 conference summaries she studied took the form of a narrative, with explicit storytelling markers, such as *first . . . then . . . next*. On closer examination, she seeks to determine how each report characterized its particular tutorial. Specifically, she asks how session notes work to construct a "good" tutorial, a "bad" one, or "one that fell somewhere in the middle" (84). With these broad categories, Malenczyk then poses more pointed questions: "What, in my writing center, constituted a 'success' narrative? Which elements seemed to be present in those 80 success narratives? And what comprised a 'failure' narrative, a story of an unsuccessful session?" (84). Malenczyk finds that

> the tutors who wrote these reports seem to characterize as "good" those sessions in which writers are well prepared, eager to learn, willing to collaborate yet also willing to take responsibility for their own work, capable of working on their own, and (perhaps most revealing) not in need of a lot of help to begin with. Those sessions they characterize as "bad" (or less than good) are those in which they perceive the students to be, well, the opposite: reluctant to work on their own, to engage in a dialogue, and perhaps in need of more help than the tutor can provide in one session. (88)

Together, the narratives of tutor reports in Malenczyk's writing center construct an uncomfortable organizational story, in which some students—the well-prepared, engaged, and cooperative—are welcomed, while others—the ill-prepared, resistant, and especially needy—are marginalized. Malenczyk speculates that, in spite of our rich literature on diversity, a number of canonical texts in tutor education encourage the deficit-model thinking that characterizes "difficult" writing center clients. "I would suggest," she writes, "that we begin to rethink our education of tutors so that it comes to represent, and help tutors think about, those students in a less . . . 'different' way" (91). She recommends that we identify and challenge institutional narratives which, like those in the session notes of failed tutoring encounters, traffic in deficit thinking and thereby impede the learning of students characterized as problematic.

CODING FOR COMMON RHETORICAL MOVES

Malenczyk's study of tutor reports offers a much-needed analysis of the content of these everyday writing center documents. In what follows, I examine session notes from my own writing center, with a similar aim of content analysis, but with a broader focus than Malenczyk's. Rather than rank consultations and their accompanying notes as "good," "bad," or "somewhere in between," my purpose at the outset was to avoid judgment explicitly and to focus, instead, on rich, detailed description of the work of conference summaries. Rather than seek out predetermined moves, using the principles of grounded theory, I took an inductive approach to analyzing session notes, looking for repeated rhetorical patterns of significance (Birks and Mills 2015; Charmaz 2014). Beginning with a small sample data set of just fifty notes, selected at random from our TutorTrac archive, I set out to identify and code recurring rhetorical moves as they emerged from the data. An initial pass yielded thirty codes. Such a large number, it seemed, would quickly become unwieldy to apply to a larger data set. And so I worked to group like patterns together, finally condensing to ten. Not surprisingly, these commonplace moves in session notes reflect a number of the "valued practices" of tutoring examined in chapter 2.

The next step was to describe each category, then select illustrative examples of each rhetorical move from the data. To test my coding scheme, two readers tried it out independently on the same set of fifty notes, making numerous suggestions for revision and refinement, resulting in the rhetorical moves, descriptions, and examples listed in table 4.1. Each code is assigned a number 1–10 to facilitate the process of coding. To underscore, these moves and excerpts are not selected because they represent either "effective" or "ineffective" commonplaces. Rather, they are typical or representative of tutor reports composed in our writing center context. To complicate the work of coding, some moves may fit persuasively into more than one category. As a

Table 4.1. Coding Scheme for Rhetorical Moves

Common Rhetorical Moves	Explanation	Examples
1 Summarize	Tutors recount the work of the consultation.	"Here's a brief summary of what we discussed today." "At your visit tonight, we went over how to format references for your APA reference list." "This morning we reviewed a draft of your conceptual metaphor paper. We also reviewed formats for APA-style citations."
2 Recommend next steps	Tutors offer suggestions for what the writer should do after the consultation, or remind the writer to follow through with recommendations discussed during the consultation.	"For the first question, add the sentences we drafted during our consultation." "We identified two places you might be able to add examples of integrity from your own life, so start there and see what more you can come up with." "I think the Robotics Club is a good place to start, and also try to get in contact with whoever sends out mass emails to the engineering students."
3 Address higher-order concerns (HOCs)	Tutors refer to work on global issues, such as content, idea development, and organization.	"This morning we worked on some organizational strategies for your thesis." "We spent today brainstorming about this subject, and came up with a brief outline. The three areas you plan to discuss are: promoting democracy abroad, protecting free trade, and global security." "There were a couple of parts in the story where you could add a little more detail, such as describing that you still wear the scar on your right hand."
4 Address lower-order concerns (LOCs)	Tutors refer to work on sentence-level errors in grammar, punctuation, and mechanics.	"Articles: We noticed that articles are still missing, and we worked on locating them." "Remember the difference between a hyphen (half-baked) and a dash (I like milk—but I don't like eggs)." "Since I was also unfamiliar with the passive voice, we went over the Passive Voice handout the UWC provides as a resource and we identified a few places in your paper when you did not write who or what was performing the action of the verb. Read through that handout before you proofread your final draft and you should be able to easily identify the passive voice."

continued on next page

Table 4.1—*continued*

Common Rhetorical Moves	Explanation	Examples
5 Offer general writing advice	Tutors make broad, unspecific, vague recommendations about writing, which may apply to any writing, regardless of context.	"If you're ever stuck, just write down anything and everything you know about the subject on a sheet of paper." "If you have a qualifying section or statement in any paper, it is better to put it at the end. Integrating into your findings gives the audience too much information to juggle at one time." "Remember to proofread, and do not rely on spell check."
6 Offer specific writing advice	Tutors make recommendations about the particular writing task discussed during the consultation, unique to its specific context.	"For your experience in Peru, for instance, explicitly state that connection between the close residence situation of the dorms there and what you'd expect to work with as an RA." "My main suggestion today is to add more description on how your listed influences impact(ed) you, your writing style, your views on music-making, etc. I get that they are awesome, but why do they matter to YOU?" "For your central idea, we came up with the question of 'How did changes in the global and local conditions of the war during the New England, Mid-Atlantic, and Southern Phases impact the American Revolution?'"
7 Recommend writing resources	Writing resources may include print and online sources, such as handouts and style guides, as well as assignment sheets, rubrics, and course materials. Resources may also include original examples generated by the tutor.	"I tried to explain the 'I before E' concept, but I forgot the finer points of the rule. Here's a website that explains it a little better: http://www.factmonster.com/ipka/A0903395.html." "Remember the difference between a hyphen (half-baked) and a dash (I like milk—but I don't like eggs)." "P.S. Bring your rubric on Wednesday so we can make sure your assignment matches it! =)."
8 Redirect	Tutors encourage writers to seek additional assistance from a teacher, classmate, another tutor, or friend.	"Ask your professor about her comments on your draft, which we marked because we weren't sure how to interpret." "Maybe you can also ask fellow classmates how they understand the assignment and the concepts in the article." "When you work with Nina for your Wed. appointment in the Writing Center, ask her about the format for the nursing care plan, because she's a nursing major too."

continued on next page

Table 4.1—*continued*

Common Rhetorical Moves	Explanation	Examples
9 Address tutoring/learning over time	Tutors reference the work of previous consultations or suggest plans for subsequent tutorials. They may encourage a follow-up consultation. Tutors may also comment on learning the writer has demonstrated over time.	"The portion of the paper that you wrote after our consultation last week did not have a lot of the problems that we worked on, which is great. You're making really great progress." "If you need help developing your next paper, you can bring some ideas when we meet again on Tuesday." "Great job on the revisions from the last consultation. The descriptions you added are much clearer now."
10 Build rapport	Tutors thank the writer for visiting the Writing Center. They offer praise or encouragement. Tutors may also express empathy or forge a personal connection.	"Ha sido un gran placer de conocerte y ayudarte con tus memorias. Espero que nos vemos de nuevo. Hasta luego!" (It's been a great pleasure to know you and help you with your memoirs. I hope we'll see you again. See you later!) "You also caught many mistakes on your own, and were able to correct them without my help. You're definitely getting better and you're learning to become your own editor, which is an invaluable skill to have." "The topic you've chosen for your research paper is very interesting! It can be intimidating to start working on a first draft for a long research paper, so feel free to make another appointment with us at the UWC!"

result, segmenting the data, so that each example is limited to the specific code it is meant to represent, is challenging. For instance, take a look at this example of "Recommend next steps": "I think the Robotics Club is a good place to start, and also try to get in contact with whoever sends out mass emails to the engineering students." While this utterance makes a recommendation, at the same time, it also points to the need to develop the essay's content, a higher-order concern. Coding session notes is further complicated because the same rhetorical move may appear, and thus need to be counted, multiple times within the same report.

As I continued to study the initial data set of fifty notes, in addition to these ten rhetorical moves, I identified another category of interest. Through the enactment of these commonplace moves, tutors seemed to me to construct distinctive identities for themselves—and, by extension, the writing center as a campus institution. Drawing on the work of Elizabeth Birr Moje, Allan Luke, Bronwyn Davies, and Brian Street

(2009), "texts and the literate practices that accompany them not only reflect but may also produce, the self" (Moje et al. 2009, 416). Initially, I found three recurring tutor roles, identities, or self-presentations, which are listed in table 4.2. Later, while coding the larger data set, I discovered that I needed to add a fourth category, "Indeterminate."

With a workable coding scheme, I gathered at random 10 percent of the session notes composed in our writing center over two semesters, for a data set of seven hundred reports. Then I met together with two more readers, one an experienced tutor, and another a novice, to teach them to code. First we used samples from the initial data set of fifty to practice on. Here, for example, is how we coded two of the session notes that open this chapter:

Session Note 2:

Hello Walley,

Thanks for coming into the UWC today. (10) Here is brief summary of our consultation. (1) You brought in your memoirs about your time in the ROTC from 1968 to 1972. Your two main concerns were that you wanted your memoirs to sound as if we were sitting down at a bar and you were telling me a story. (3) Furthermore, you wanted your memoirs to be free of any grammatical errors before being published. (4)

Overall, your memoirs sound great! The story captivated me and I would love to finish reading it when you have finished the final chapter. (10) (12)

However, we did observe that there were some issues with comma placement. We went over some sentences that needed commas and you were able to identify where the commas should go with little of my assistance. (1) (4) (11) I gave you a great handout about commas that I recommend you utilize when you continue editing the memoirs. (7)

Additionally, when you see places where you use parenthesis, consider whether or not they are necessary and if they can be eliminated. (4) (2) (5) I think it will make your story sound more fluent.

Lastly, look over the notes that we took on the two copies of the draft. (2) Cannot wait to read the finished copy! (12) Que te vaya bien mi amigo y que tengas un buen viaje. (10)

Sinceramente,

J.R.

Table 4.2. Coding Scheme for Tutor Roles

Tutor Roles	Explanation	Examples
11 Peer collaborator / co-learner	Tutors use repeated "we" language to describe the work writer and tutor accomplished together. Tutors may recount joint answer seeking and problem solving during the consultation. Tutors may also note the limits of their knowledge or expertise.	"We tried to cut for content as we went, but I was a bit hesitant to cut for wordiness, not knowing the conventions of scientific writing. Definitely ask your professor to help with this when you submit it to her for review."
		"We looked into topics to discuss within these areas, including the sanctions against Iran, the war in Afghanistan, the global war on terrorism, and the Somali pirate seizures."
		"I'll do some more research on business-style writing so I will be able to help you analyze your response next week."
12 Interested reader	Tutors express interest and engagement, as readers, in the writer's text.	"I think your story sounds great; it is very detailed. I look forward to reading that missing page when you send me the final copy via email."
		"I really loved the scene of W. and B. hiding out from the enemy, and the fight scene. They were excellently done. They really got my heartbeat up and I found myself holding my breath."
		"The story captivated me and I would love to finish reading it when you have finished the final chapter."
13 Teacher/authority	Tutors make authoritative pronouncements about rules and conventions for writing. They may also offer teacherly evaluation of the writer and/or text.	"Grammar: In your Everyday Writer handbook you can find the grammar and punctuation section, which I showed you on page 326. Focus on the green box labeled 'At a glance' for more information on common grammatical errors."
		"The introduction to your Significance and Background section should only describe, in general terms, what you are going to talk about. Leave the specifics for later."
		"As a whole, the story is working really well. Great job!"
14 Indeterminate	Tutor's role does not appear to fit one or more of the three categories above.	

Session Note 4:

Hey Victoria, thanks for coming to the University Writing Center! (10)
Here's a brief summary of what we discussed today, I hope it helps (1):

Longman Dictionary: Some of the word choices that you have made
do not necessarily relate to the message you are trying to explain. (4)
This can be caused by several reasons; I want to focus on how you can
get a better understanding of these words. By using *Longman Dictionary*, words not only simplified but explained when the use of the word
would be proper. Here is the website: http://www.ldoceonline.com/.
(7)

Articles: We discussed how you were missing some articles. The omission of these articles can, and will, have an effect on how a reader understands your message. (4) The worksheet I have given you is designed
to clarify various misunderstanding. (7)

Readability/Grammar: Your understanding of the English language
is very strong, more so than my own! I want to congratulate you for that
accomplishment. (10) The words has/have/ had obviously gave you
an issue when writing them. Pay attention to how you are using these
words. (4)

Overall, I felt that the reflection piece was very strong. (13) Although we weren't able to start reading the actual annotated bib. due
to time constraints, I hope that what we did touch on can help you better revise your overall paper. (10)

Best Wishes,

V.

After some practice, we turned our attention to the larger data set.
One third of the data we coded collaboratively, discussing options,
debating decisions, talking to consensus. After calibrating our coding
by working together, the two readers divided another third of the data
between themselves to code independently, highlighting troublesome
instances for further discussion when we met next. The last third of the
data I coded myself alone.

While much of our coding was relatively straightforward, the vexing instances that prompted disagreement or just plain confusion led
to rich, generative talk about both our interpretative practices and the
challenges of composing conference summaries. Here is one example
of a tutor report that tripped up all three of us:

Session Note 5:

Hey Marcul! Thanks for stopping in today. I appreciated your clarity and thoughts; you write in a very understandable way, but made the topic interesting. Here are the notes from our session today: 1) (possible) give an author's perception on each missed opportunity 2) finish China/write Indochina 3) mention Collins in Indochina section 4) why/how Gaddis is least sympathetic 5) why/how Herring is less sympathetic 6) why/how Kisinger is most sympathetic 7) tie in the assessment to each "sympathetic" section (see third point in professor's email) 8) conclusion: thesis + content (see handout) 9) add source citations Also Purdue OWL is the site we talked about for all citing help! Good luck:) -S.

More than usual among session notes, this one seems to depend for its meaning on a shared insider understanding between tutor and writer of the content of the consultation. As outside readers, we weren't certain how to make sense of the work described here. We had difficulty deciding what to do with the numbered items: should we read and code them as distinct activities, different issues worked on during the consultation? Or should we understand them collectively, as subsets of a larger whole, which appears to be aimed mainly at generating ideas and putting them into some recognizable organizational pattern? This instance highlights a persistent challenge we encountered in coding tutor reports: deciding how to segment the data. Notes are not easily divided so that each segment yields only a single code. Codes overlap. And occasionally, as in this instance, the work described appears opaque. The best we could figure in this case is that this note shows evidence of—we think— building rapport, summarizing the work of the consultation, recommending next steps, addressing higher-order concerns, offering specific writing advice, and recommending resources. How many times each of these moves is enacted remains unclear.

This inquiry into a large number and variety of session notes led my fellow coders and me to remark repeatedly during our coding and debriefing sessions that this activity prompted us to think more reflectively about how we go about composing session notes. These conversations also led us to think about the processes currently in place in our writing center, and additional scaffolding that might be added in the future, to guide tutors to learn to write more effective session notes.

SOME FINDINGS

Although we sometimes disagreed, in the main, our coding was remarkably consistent. Likewise, across two semesters we found consistent patterns, even while our writing center experienced significant turnover in staff across the two terms, with a number of tutors graduating and a new cohort of twenty novices added during that time. This consistency across an unstable population of peer consultants suggests that while tutors may come and go, there are some stable-for-now norms for composing tutor reports within our writing center community of practice. Our analysis appears in figure 4.1. Keep in mind that because the same rhetorical moves may appear multiple times within the same tutor report, the scale on the graph exceeds the number of seven hundred individual notes selected for study.

We found several noteworthy trends in the data. First, by far the most frequent rhetorical move is "build rapport," with 1,040 instances. Having directed three different writing centers over the past fifteen years, I'm struck by the rapport-building moves that characterize session notes in the Writing Center at UCF. While session notes may have multiple audiences, including writers, teachers, tutors, and administrators, consultants in this writing center show a marked preference for emphasizing the student writer as the primary audience. Session notes are a direct person-to-person communication between peer tutors and writers. The frequency of rapport-building moves reflects this norm. By contrast, in my first writing center, in which tutor reports were logged on 5×7 blue index cards and housed in a small metal file box, the primary audience was tutors themselves, so that they could consult a writer's record to gather information about prior work before beginning a new consultation. Writers and teachers seldom saw these records, unless they asked for them. Tutors wrote mainly to an audience of other tutors, with no need to build rapport.

I encountered yet a third norm when I arrived to my second writing center. There, a strong culture of reporting directly to teachers was well established. In session notes, tutors wrote *about* writers, not *to* them. Likewise, with a primary purpose of documenting work, not building relationships, the tone of these reports to teachers tended to be more formal. Because this writing center sidestepped writers to communicate directly with their teachers, tutor reports occasionally included negative evaluations of writers themselves. As these three different approaches to conference summaries illustrate, norms around session notes both reflect and reproduce the institutional cultures and values of which they are a part.

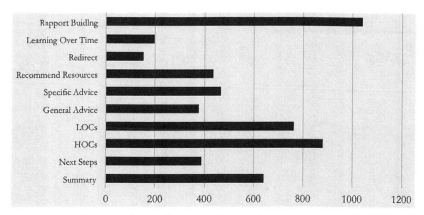

Figure 4.1. Ten Common Rhetorical Moves in Session Notes

Our analysis showed that the least common rhetorical move is "redirecting" the writer to seek additional assistance from a teacher, classmate, another tutor, or friend, with only 154 instances. Even so, this is a move I'm happy to see at all, for it reflects another core value in our writing center, where we work to discourage tutors from performing as "experts." Even when a tutor *does* know, playing the role of expert too often leads to missed opportunities for the writer to engage in learning. Leading with ignorance, on the other hand, creates its own problems, namely that it undermines the writer's confidence in the tutor. Peer tutors need to strike a balance between appearing to know either too much or too little. They need to be willing to say, "I don't know." Ideally, this admission ought to be followed with, "But I can help you find out." This puts the focus of tutoring not on what the tutor does—or doesn't—know, but, instead, on joint problem solving between writer and tutor. In short, redirecting is a move that acknowledges that the tutor is not an authority, reminding writers to leverage the full complement of human resources available to support their writing development.

Another positive sign we found in the data is that attention to higher-order concerns (880 instances) slightly outstrips the focus on lower-order concerns (763 instances). For those who would chide writing centers for not giving enough attention to matters of correctness, this data confirms that, at least in conference summaries composed in our writing center, tutors spend quite a lot of time addressing grammar, punctuation, and mechanics. At the same time, while writers want and need and should receive help learning to proofread and edit, the slightly higher emphasis on global concerns reflects the commonplace writing center assumption that content and organization need attention *before* (not instead of) matters of correctness and style.

Related to this, I think, are the rhetorical moves of offering "specific writing advice" (466 instances) and "general writing advice" (377 instances). General recommendations, which may apply to any writing, regardless of context, such as the finger-wagging admonition, "Watch your comma use!" aren't particularly meaningful. By contrast, concrete, specific recommendations that emerge from the collaborative work on a particular writing task, such as a sample thesis sentence, are potentially useful. But this noses beyond the scope of the current study into the reception of tutor reports. In the next phase of research we need to learn from writers themselves what kinds of suggestions they find useful, and what, exactly, makes them so.

Next, I'd like to consider the rhetorical move "address tutoring/ learning over time" (198 instances). A few short years ago, the majority of students visited our writing center, on average, two to three times. Only in the past year, with a number of strategic efforts, have we begun to see an emerging trend of more recurring consultations. Because learning happens gradually over time, to make more productive use of the writing center, writers need to visit more frequently throughout the writing process, and across multiple writing tasks. Tutors "address tutoring/learning over time," in part, by inviting writers, explicitly, to return to the writing center.

While our findings tell us the frequency of this move, they don't tell us anything about the *quality* of such invitations. "Come back anytime!" sounds like empty, customer-service patter to me. By contrast, "When you visit again on Tues., bring your assignment directions so that we can check to see that you've met all the requirements" highlights a particular purpose for a specific follow-up tutorial. What, we might ask writers, are the consequences of various *kinds* of invitations and directives like these? Further, via the same move, tutors use session notes not only to sum up the work of the consultation at hand, but also to address the writer's long-term learning goals, progress, and development across multiple consultations. I'd like to keep an eye on this pattern going forward to find out if it correlates with the rising number of repeat visits.

Similarly, with a recent master's thesis on the use of writing resources during consultations, attention in our writing center has increased of late on this aspect of tutoring (Lambert 2015). "Recommend writing resources" (435 instances) is another rhetorical move that, I suspect, may be on the rise. Tracking over time would reveal if this is the case. With it, tutors use the session notes to extend the support of the tutorial, often reminding writers of resources used during the consultation, but also frequently introducing new resources not previously discussed, either to provide help for a concern that was not addressed during the consultation, or to amend or extend information that was discussed. Like "redirecting," this move underscores that knowledge is not merely *in* the tutor as authoritative writing consultant; rather, it is distributed among a variety of tools, including various writing resources. This move, I think, reflects a commonplace assumption that the role of an effective tutor is not simply to tell or give answers, but, instead, to help writers to learn to find answers for themselves. Directing writers to resources is one way to model this behavior.

Finally, on average, we found that over half of the session notes explicitly address next steps the writer should take following the consultation (388 instances). This is a circumstance to be regarded positively, if you're a glass-half-full sort of reader. A more pessimistic interpretation would note that nearly half of the conference summaries fail to mention next steps. While the majority of tutor reports make some move to sum up the work of the consultation (641 instances), summing up is primarily an accountability move. Summing up provides evidence of the writer's work in the writing center, which might be especially useful to teachers who require writing center use, or reward a visit with extra credit. But for the writer herself, summing up may be less useful than detailing what next steps she should engage *after* the consultation. This mixed picture makes me inclined to urge tutors to place more emphasis on detailing next steps, and perhaps to see this as the primary goal of conference summaries.

Figure 4.2 illustrates our findings from the second category of interest in the session notes, recurring tutor roles, identities, or self-presentations.

Well over half of tutor presentations, 408, were coded as "peer collaborator/co-learner." Given the emphasis in our writing center on peer-with-peer learning this value reflected in the session notes is encouraging. By contrast, only 182 sessions were coded as characterized by a tutor role of teacher/authority. Interestingly, this category was one where the two student coders and I disagreed more frequently, with only 60 percent agreement in our coding of tutor identities. In general, the peer tutors tended to see more peerness enacted, whereas I tended to see more teacher/authority moves on the part of tutors. While "interested reader" ranked high in our initial sample of fifty notes, in the larger data set this tutor identity appeared only thirty-six times.

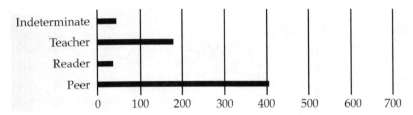

Figure 4.2. Four Common Tutor Roles

CONCEPTUAL FRAMEWORK: DISCOURSE ANALYSIS

Jackie Grutsch McKinney (2016) points out in *Strategies for Writing Center Research* that "One of the most common strategies for studying writing center work . . . is discourse analysis. **Discourse analysis** is the study of language in use—in written, gestural, or oral form" (39; emphasis in original). To further analyze the rhetorical moves of session notes, this chapter draws on approaches to discourse analysis offered by James Paul Gee (2014). *In How to Do Discourse Analysis: A Toolkit*, Gee details twenty-eight tools for conducting discourse analysis, any number of which might be applicable. Here, to illustrate, I focus on just three, which are particularly useful for explicating the discoursal work of tutor reports.

As Gee (2005) puts it, "Whenever we speak or write, we always and simultaneously build one of seven things or seven areas of 'reality.' We often build more than one of these simultaneously through the same words and deeds. Let's call these seven things," Gee proposes, "the 'seven building tasks' of language in use. In turn, since we use language to build these seven things, a discourse analyst can ask seven different questions about any piece of language-in-use. This gives us, in turn, seven . . . tools for discourse analysis" (94). Among these seven building tools are the three I'll put to use in the analysis that follows: the "identities" building tool, the "relationships" building tool, and the "politics" or "social goods" building tool (112–29).

Naming and counting the rhetorical moves tutors make in session notes is only a first step to understanding the work tutor reports do. Discourse analysis allows for a more detailed interpretation of these moves and what they accomplish rhetorically. In particular, as our analysis of the data above suggests, session notes give rise to specific tutor identities. To make sense of this identity work, Gee (2014) proposes:

> For any communication, ask what socially recognizable identity or identities the speaker is trying to enact or to get others to recognize. Ask also how the speaker's language treats other people's identities, what sorts of identities the speaker recognizes for others in relationship to his or her

own. Ask, too, how the speaker is positioning others, what identities the speaker is "inviting" them to take up. (116)

To return to Session Note 1, which opens this chapter, for example, notice the prevalence of "we" language: "Tonight we looked at," "Most of what we discussed," "We came up with the question," "We discussed organizing your discussion." This accumulation of "we" statements constructs a tutor identity as peer collaborator and co-learner. Reema, the tutor, positions herself as co-author to Sari, the writer. What's more, Reema's framing of the work implies agreement, and thus a smooth and cooperative relationship between the two. Further constructing her identity through language, Reema repeatedly mitigates her authority as tutor. For instance, to set up her recommendations, she downplays her directives, not as imperatives, but "as a reminder," "some key points to think about." Through her language, Reema constructs herself, not a teacher telling a writer what to do, but as a fellow student who has engaged in joint problem solving and production together with the writer to discover options, suggestions. Further minimizing her authority, Reema redirects Sari, to "Check with your professor." As peer tutor, Reema is not an all-knowing expert. Her closing, "Best of luck with your paper, and thank you for visiting the Writing Center!" also puts Reema in a deferential posture. While a professor, whose power position differs markedly from that of a peer tutor's, would not likely thank a student for visiting during office hours, Reema constructs herself as a grateful service worker, echoing the sort of customer-service language we might expect to hear in a hospitality or retail setting. Her final exclamation point underscores the role of the happy, enthusiastic customer-service provider. This closing exclamation invites us to consider how to read the other two exclamations in the same session note, both of which follow a directive: "Thesis that can address an overarching question!" and "Outline to get your ideas out!" Out of context, a reader might wonder if Reema is screaming commands at Sari. But read alongside the closing, Reema seems, rather, to voice a boisterous enthusiasm, which characterizes both the role of interested, engaged, peer collaborator and jovial customer-service worker.

Such identity work is intimately tied to establishing and maintaining relationships. Given the prevalence of rapport-building moves across the corpus of session notes, this is a significant move to attend to. To apply the relationship building tool, Gee advises: "For any communication, ask how words and various grammatical devices are being used to build and sustain or change relationships of various sorts among the speaker, other people, social groups, cultures, and/or institutions"

(121). Turning to Session Note 2, we can see several key relationship-building moves on the part of J. R., the tutor, toward Walley, the writer. The friendly, informal salutation, "Hello Walley," sets the tone for what follows. In the first paragraph, the prevalence of "you" language is striking: "You brought in your memoirs," "Your two main concerns were," "you wanted your memoirs to sound as if we were sitting down at a bar and you were telling me a story," "you wanted your memoirs free of any grammatical errors." One the one hand, this accumulation of "you" statements constructs an identity for J. R. as an active listener, who attends carefully to Walley's concerns and, to demonstrate that, paraphrases them back afterwards in his session note. As Gee (2014) reminds us, "Identity and relationships go hand in hand." For the purposes of conducting discourse analysis, however, he recommends disentangling the two: "Creating and taking on identity and creating and sustaining a relationship of a certain type are not the same, however closely related they are. Identities set up parameters for a relationship" (121). For J. R. and Walley this is the first of three consultations that take place over as many weeks. From the start, the two strike up an easy rapport, which includes discussion of Walley's first language, Spanish. J. R., a native English speaker, is studying Spanish, and so frequently they switch back and forth between the two languages during tutoring. In his session notes, J. R. takes further steps to forge a relationship with Walley, based on shared language, ending each with a closing in Spanish. Thus, Walley becomes "mi amigo." Neither peer collaborator nor authoritative teacher, J. R., instead, uses language to construct a primary identity as interested reader: "The story captivated me and I would love to finish reading it when you have finished the chapter," he writes. Later, he underscores, enthusiastically, "Cannot wait to read the finished copy!" Yet, we see conflict in J. R.'s role. The praise he gives with the one hand, he then qualifies with the other, in typical teacher fashion: "However, we did observe that there were some issues with comma placement." The same teacherly advisor recommends later, "Additionally, when you see places where you use parentheses, consider whether or not they are necessary and if they can be eliminated." This shift from what "we" observed together to what "you" must learn to see independently reflects J. R.'s approach to tutoring, first scaffolding the work through modeling and joint production, then pushing the writer toward greater independence. "*We* went over some sentences that needed commas," he reminds Walley, "and *you* were able to identify where the commas should go with little of my assistance" (emphasis added) J. R.'s focus here is less on Walley's deficits, more on what he *can* do. In this way, J. R. constructs an identity for Walley as a capable, engaged writer, willing to revise. To end, with a nod toward Walley's upcoming trip to Colombia ("y que tengas un buen viaje"), J. R. uses language to express interest in Walley's life beyond the narrow confines of the writing center consultation, and thus to cement their relationship as one based on more than just talk about writing.

In addition to the identity work and relationship building of session notes, Gee's (2014) "politics" building tool draws our attention to what he terms "social goods" (124). Gee explains: "By 'politics,' I mean, not government and political parties, but any situation in which the distribution of social goods is at stake. By 'social goods' I mean anything a social group or society takes as a good worth having." One good worth having in our writing center is the valued practices for tutoring enumerated in chapter 2. One way to understand the discourse of session notes is to read them through the lens of these practices. While observations of tutoring give us one way to see the extent to which tutors enact these values, session notes, too, are another window into the ways tutors do— or don't—engage them, and construct stories about valued practices via session notes. Gee (2014) advises:

> For any communication, ask how words and grammatical devices are being used to build (construct, assume) what counts as a social good and to distribute this good or to withhold it from listeners or others. Ask, as well, how words and grammatical devices are being used to build a viewpoint on how social goods are or should be distributed in society. (126)

If we consider our "20 Valued Practices for Tutoring Writing" as social goods, then we might notice, for example, the ways the tutor in Session Note 3 above uses language to highlight certain values. Valued practice number nine, for instance, directs tutors to "Prioritize global concerns that interfere with meaning before less significant local errors in grammar, punctuation, and mechanics." In this note, Shane, the tutor, leads with "We tried to cut for content," underscoring the value of prioritizing higher order concerns before lower order. But both he and the writer are uncertain, however, about how to interpret one of the questions in Sarah's scholarship application. To account for their conflicting understandings, Shane recommends, still focusing on content before correctness, "We decided your best course of action would be to write out answers for both possible interpretations." Only in his final suggestion does Shane tackle a sentence-level concern: "Also, once you've finished your draft, pay attention to introductory commas in your revisions." Here, not only does Shane himself set this as a later priority, but he also works to persuade the writer, too, that correctness should be addressed only after completing a rough draft. Also in keeping with our writing center's valued practices for tutoring, number nineteen on our list advises, "Be willing to say, 'I don't know.' Don't pretend expertise." With this social good in mind, Shane twice redirects Sarah to the chair of her honors in the major thesis committee for expert advice: "Definitely ask your professor to help with this" and, later, "She probably knows best what this application requires, so definitely trust her advice on this."

While the primary purpose of this chapter is to construct a big-picture view of commonplace rhetorical moves and tutor identities exhibited across a large corpus of session notes selected at random from our local writing center context, these brief forays into Gee's *How to Do Discourse Analysis* demonstrate up close some of the ways session notes bring Gee's building tasks into being. Further work using discourse analysis promises an even richer, more detailed description of the work of conference summaries.

REFLECTING AND CONSTRUCTING UNDERLYING VALUES AND ASSUMPTIONS

As our analysis shows, session notes both reflect and construct the underpinning values and institutional ethos of a writing center, including its tutoring practices. With that in mind, the specific themes I've examined here are less important, I think, than the *activity* of inquiry into the work of conference summaries. After all, while the ten commonplace rhetorical moves and three tutor identities examined here would be recognizable in most writing centers, they are not universal. And they need not be. My aim is not to argue what work conference summaries *should* do. To echo Kim Jackson (1996), "While I want to underscore that I don't believe there is an 'ideal' format or practice, I do believe that the follow-up approaches used by a writing center must be in line with the aims and goals of that particular writing center" (11). While writing centers may share some basic principles, to some extent, all writing centers are local. And so the common rhetorical moves and tutor identities we find in our session notes may be quite different from those you find in yours. My point is that you won't know until you look. As I hope this book demonstrates, chapter after chapter, the act of inquiry—and the generative talk and thinking that this looking prompts—is where the magic happens. In the case of our writing center, inquiry into tutor reports has lead not only to further research, but also to renewed efforts to teach this unfamiliar genre to tutors explicitly, now from a new position of deeper knowledge about what, exactly, the work of session notes in our writing center actually looks like. To that end, I conclude this chapter with an assignment I designed to engage peer tutors in studying and coding their own session notes. Such an assignment is one way to start a conversation about the work of conference summaries, the values they reflect and enact, and why that work and those values matter.

ASSIGNMENT: CODING SAMPLES OF YOUR SESSION NOTES

To understand the work of writing center session notes, we need to begin by looking closely at representative samples, asking, "What are the commonplace rhetorical moves we find in session notes?" Our goal is to identify significant repeated patterns, moves that we can point to and label again and again, in a systematic way, across multiple examples of session notes.

Once we identify patterns of common rhetorical moves, then we can count and compare, determining which moves are more or less common than others.

Then we can ask, "Are these the moves session notes *should* make?" "Should some moves be *more* or *less* frequent?" "Or are their *other* moves that we don't find, but that we ought to make instead?"

To fully understand the work of session notes, we need next to survey and interview tutees themselves, to learn what meanings they make of the session notes they receive, and how they use them to revise and develop as writers. But that's another data set. For this small assignment, let's look closely at examples of session notes you and colleagues in our writing center have composed to determine what work they're doing.

To Do:

Select, copy, and paste three to four recent session notes of your own into a Word document.

Then use the coding scheme described above in **tables 4.1 and 4.2** to identify the same rhetorical moves and tutor identities in your own session notes. (These moves are ones I've identified by studying hundreds of session notes at random from our writing center.) To code your notes, write the number on your notes where you find the move. Use the sample excerpts I've provided next to each code to help you find comparable moves in your own notes. To model coding for you, I've included two samples, **Session Notes 2** and **4** above, with numbered codes inserted into the texts in parentheses.

As you look for the patterns I've identified, also keep your eye out for significant patterns I've *not* named here. If you find a move that you think is particularly noteworthy, create a new corresponding code, explanation, and example of your own. To be worthy of a new code, the move needs to be (1) repeated frequently across multiple notes, (2) significant, and (3) distinct from the other moves already coded for.

After you've coded your own notes, swap with a partner. Without sharing the results of your own coding, code each other's session notes independently. Then compare and discuss to see how similar or divergent your coding is from your partner's. If the codes are robust, then we should come to agreement most of the time. In other words, no matter who is interpreting the session notes, the codes ought to be relatively consistent.

With every consultant coding a selection of notes, we'll be able to see broadly the moves that characterize session notes across our writing center community of practice.

Questions for Discussion and Reflection:

1. What commonplace rhetorical moves and tutor roles do you find in your session notes?

2. To what extent do the codes provided in tables 4.1 and 4.2 adequately describe the work of your conference summaries? What, if any, other significant patterns do you find in your notes?

3. What values and assumptions are reflected in session notes?

4. In what ways does examining the repeated patterns in your session notes lead you to reflect on your approach to these reports? What have you learned or thought about as a result of this activity that might lead you to compose session notes differently going forward?

5. What more do you need to learn in order to write effective session notes?

5

BLOGGING AS A TOOL FOR DIALOGIC REFLECTION[1]

*In an age of collective intelligence rather than individual expertise,
it is crucial to resource collective intelligence through smart tools that
allow groups to learn, design, produce, and solve problems. These tools
must be "owned" by the group in the sense that they can adapt the tools,
transform them, mentor others in their use, and integrate them into
their social organization.*

—James Paul Gee (2013), *The Anti-Education Era:
Creating Smarter Students Through Digital Learning*

IN THIS CHAPTER

- **Focal Documents:** excerpts from a local, internal writing center blog
- **Purpose:** to engage tutors in dialogic reflection about tutoring theory and practice
- **Conceptual Framework for Analysis:** reflective practice
- **Data:** posts, comments, and other reflective writing from tutors
- **Assignment:** "Assess Your Thinking, Writing, and Learning on the Blog"

In chapter 2, by examining the document "20 Valued Practices for Tutoring Writing" through the lens of a "communities of practice" conceptual framework, we saw the part this document plays in establishing a shared repertoire of tutoring strategies. In this chapter, the same theory works adjacently with another framework, "reflective practice" to illuminate the ways an internal blog operates similarly, to establish and maintain a writing center culture of reflective writing, thinking, and tutoring practice. In this way, I hope to show how these two theoretical perspectives work in complimentary fashion to support the work of tutor education.

CONCEPTUAL FRAMEWORK: TUTORING WRITING AS REFLECTIVE PRACTICE

As George Hillocks (1995) argues in *Teaching Writing as Reflective Practice*, reflection is an essential habit of mind for effective teaching and learning:

DOI: 10.7330/9781607325826.c005

> Active critical reflection is necessary in every aspect of our teaching, not
> only in front of the class. We must try to reevaluate our own values and
> experiences as they relate to our teaching. Our assumptions and theories
> about teaching composition must remain open to inspection, evaluation,
> and revision, a condition that requires an active inquiry paralleling the
> inquiry in which we engage our students. (217)

Here Hillocks draws a connection between inquiry and theory in the
sense of unacknowledged or implicit values, assumptions, and beliefs
that underlie everyday routines. Reflective thinking, in Hillocks's view,
is bound up with both theorizing our work and with an inquiry stance.
Valued for prompting tutors to engage in self-assessment, to expand
their repertoire of strategies, and to improve their practice, reflective
writing has long been a cornerstone of writing center tutor education (Bell 2001; Mattison 2007; Okawa et al. 1991; Smith 2005; Yancey
2002). Through critical reflection, theories and decisions remain open
to inspection, evaluation, and revision. Reflection is dogged, however,
by two problems. First, its audience is typically limited to the self and
to the writing center director. This limited audience leads to a second
problem: limited learning. What's more, underlying reflection is the
assumption that one has an informed critical framework already in place
for thinking about tutoring practices. Kathleen Blake Yancey (2002) in
"Seeing Practice Through Their Eyes: Reflection as Teacher" includes
several excerpts from tutors' reflective writing, which bring to mind
Romantic notions of the self. In this excerpt, the tutor asserts her own
private being as a special entity transcending the normal run of tutors.
She sets her own personal drama against the broader workings of the
writing center community:

> Now that my time in the WRC [Writing Resources Center] as a tutor has
> ended, I do not see myself as a tutor; I see myself as a "Tutor." I know now
> what I should have realized all along. I am my own person with my own
> distinct style and personality; so therefore, I am not a robot that has come
> off the assembly line with all of the information I need to become a tutor.
> I am an individual who is different from all other Tutors in the WRC. I
> have a style that works best for me, and there is not a book anywhere that
> can tell me what this style is or should be. I am a Tutor, who knows the
> theory behind the writing conference and is confident enough to take this
> knowledge and weave my own individualism into it. (197–98)

If this tutor experiences an authentic audience for her reflective writing, it is the writing center director. Not only is her audience truncated,
but also, in setting herself apart from her writing center colleagues, this
consultant cuts herself off from the multiple conceptual frameworks
that circulate among them and the various insights they might add to

her thinking about her tutoring experiences. Yancey says of this mode of reflection:

> I have my observations, and my interactions, too, but in some ways most important, I have *multiple documents that collectively teach me—in their own words—how tutors learn to become tutors.*
>
> I read the materials of one tutor, then of another. Soon I am learning about all of them—from their letters, their e-mails, their logs, their classroom discourse, and their inventions. (196; emphasis in original)

Yancey herself is learning about tutors, but what, one wonders, are they learning from each other? And what are they learning about their work?

Michael Mattison's (2007) "Someone to Watch Over Me: Reflection and Authority in the Writing Center" explores the problem of audience for tutors' reflective writing. In Mattison's case, tutoring practices and learning are undermined because reflective writing leads consultants to feel as though they are being spied upon by the writing center director. Surveillance, Mattison finds, directs and limits consultants' writing about their tutoring experiences. An advocate of reflection, Mattison urges a cautious approach. "[R]eflective work," he writes, "is like a sharp knife. You wouldn't try working in a kitchen without one, but you would also take care when handling it" (47). At the close of his essay, Mattison, suggests an alternative: to achieve its espoused goals, rather than an internal monologue or a one-way communication from consultant to writing center director, reflective writing ought to be recast as dialogue among tutors.

This chapter takes up Mattison's call for dialogic reflection. Via a writing center weblog, the primary document for examination, consultants use reflective writing to engage in conversation about the theory and practice of tutoring. In this way, the blog plays a critical role in tutor training and in developing a writing center community of practice. By posting reflective writing to the blog and talking with peers about it, consultants maintain and transform their writing center community as they adopt and adapt its practices; likewise, the community sustains and alters consultants through opportunities for participation and enculturation. As their blog posts illustrate, reflection-as-dialogue promotes deep theoretical understanding of writing center work, with discussion focused not only on procedural knowledge but also on explicating the values, assumptions, and beliefs, which govern tutoring practices. In other words, common sense or explication without critical engagement is insufficient. Rather, to be useful, dialogic reflection must offer more than practical advice about how to tutor. In addition to considering local knowledge generated in its particular writing center context, dialogic reflection must also take up and engage—perhaps to question and maybe even dismiss—expert knowledge generated by writing center specialists.

Central to the writing centers I have directed is the belief that, while consultants need procedural knowledge in order to work effectively, a set of how-tos is insufficient. Our tutor training, then, encourages consultants to adopt an inquiry stance toward writing center practice. Such a stance involves relentless questioning, asking *why*, wondering, researching, generating alternatives, testing, reviewing, and revising options. The purpose of inquiry is not merely to solve problems or to correct practice. Rather, its aim is to examine both what we do and the rules and reasoning—the habits of mind—that determine what we do. Chris Argyris (1991) offers the terms "single-loop" and "double-loop" learning to capture this distinction. He uses the analogy of an automatic thermostat to illustrate his point. Learning-as-problem-solving, or single-loop learning, says Argyris, works like a thermostat. Whenever the temperature drops below 68 degrees, the thermostat responds by correcting the problem and turning on the heat. By contrast, a thermostat would be engaged in double-loop learning if it could ask, "'Why am I set at 68 degrees?' and then explore whether or not some other temperature might more economically achieve the goal of heating the room" (4). Among our tutors, double-loop learning is developed, in part, through dialogic reflection.

BACKGROUND: REFLECTIVE WRITING IN ONE WRITING CENTER

A brief recent history of reflective writing in the writing center at California State University, Chico, the first writing center in which I began using the weblog, illustrates the move from single-loop to double-loop thinking. When I began as director there, my predecessor shared the ways she employed reflective writing. At the start of her tenure, she found a writing center that was, in her words, "perilously close to useless." Among other things, tutoring practices were confused, ungrounded in writing center theory and research. Consultants typically dove for the papers writers put before them, focusing almost exclusively on correcting sentence-level errors in grammar, punctuation, and mechanics, without first learning the context for writing, including the writer's understanding of the purpose, audience, and genre requirements. To help consultants to prioritize global concerns before local and to turn their attention from fixing papers to facilitating learning, my colleague developed what came to be known in that writing center as the "Session Reflection Sheet," which included the following prompt:

Use this sheet (front and back, if needed) to write a reflection on the session. Begin by explaining how you learned the context for writing, including the student's understanding of the assignment and the required genre. If you worked on sentence-level errors, explain why you made this choice and what specific strategies you used to teach the writer to proof-read and edit independently.

Tutors were required to write a session reflection after every consultation. This reflective writing, along with several other changes in the center, including a complete overhaul of the tutor-education course, proved effective. Writing assistants[2] soon developed a wide array of strategies, rooted in literacy research and theory, for developing a writer's understanding, rather than merely fixing papers. At its inception, the "Session Reflection Sheet" served another valuable function. With a writing center staffed entirely by novice consultants from the tutor-education course, which was offered every semester, new writing assistants had no experienced peers to learn from. What, newcomers wondered, semester after semester, were some effective tutoring practices common to our center? With files created for every writer, the Reflection Sheets provided case histories, which writing assistants could consult, to learn common practices. In time, the previous director successfully argued for several paid positions for experienced tutors, which she designated as "mentors." In addition to tutoring, mentors were charged with helping to train new consultants. With this development, novice writing assistants came to consult mentors more and more, and the written case histories of tutoring less and less.

Under my watch, consultants began to complain about the amount of reflective writing they were required to do. Completing a session reflection after every consultation, they insisted, was a burden. As a result, reflective writing became detached from the practice of reflective thinking and action. Tutors no longer found it a meaningful activity. Instead, the "Session Reflection Sheet" had become what Etienne Wenger (1998) calls a "reification," which is, in his words, "[G]iving form to our experience by producing objects that congeal that experience into 'thingness.' In doing so, we create points of focus around which the negotiation of meaning becomes organized" (58). Reification is neither good nor bad. It simply is. Reification, as Wenger points out, is central to every practice. "Any community of practice," he writes, "produces abstractions, tools, symbols, stories, terms, and concepts that reify something of that practice in congealed form" (59). For example, when you are called upon to write a meeting agenda, you don't have to wonder what the genre features of this form of writing are. You simply search your computer for an agenda from a previous meeting and then use it as a template. This template embodies our ideas about the form and function of an agenda. In every aspect of our lives, reifications like this facilitate action. Our writing center's "Session Reflection Sheet," however, had become a reification that undermined learning when consultants viewed it as a mindless routine.

Stubbornly, however, I maintained a castor-oil attitude toward reflective writing: it might not taste good going down, but it's good for you. Keep writing, I insisted. One semester I tried reward, paying consultants for the additional time they spent writing. Another semester I tried coercion, conducting random checks, threatening to dock the pay of tutors who skipped a dose of reflective medicine. Meanwhile, writing assistants continued to insist that session reflections had become little more than busy work. My reaction is what Argyris terms a "defensive routine" (8). Like the thermostat in his analogy, I was engaged in single-loop thinking, trying to correct reflective writing. But the way I was going about defining and solving the problem was part of the problem itself. Reflexively, I turned attention away from my own behavior and reasoning and onto that of the writing consultants, short-circuiting an opportunity for us to learn about, and perhaps revise, the application of reflection in our writing center. Rather than deny my own responsibility by externalizing the problem and putting it on the tutors, double-loop thinking called upon me to examine the principles and propositions I used to design and implement my actions.

Double-loop thinking required me to ask not only *how* to implement reflective writing effectively, but also *why*—and, further, *whether* tutors should engage in reflective writing in the first place. I began by considering my role in initiating reflective writing via the Reflection Sheet, which I had adopted, well, unreflectively. Though a well-intentioned effort to engage writing assistants in critical reflection, in practice, the prompt is itself an illustration of single-loop thinking. Its genesis was a desire to correct what the previous director and I had viewed as bad practice. Without first learning the context for writing, consultants turned their attention too quickly and narrowly to fixing sentence-level errors. Don't do that, our prompt admonishes. Instead, "Begin by explaining how you learned the context for writing, including the student's understanding of the assignment and the required genre." For the tutor who does not first learn the student's understanding of the assignment and the required genre, there is little room for an authentic response. The writing assistant must either fabricate a reflection or ignore the directive altogether. Similarly well-intended, the prompt's second sentence offers a way in: "If you worked on sentence-level errors, explain why you made this choice and what specific strategies you used to teach the writer to proofread and edit independently." The consultant who employs no specific teaching strategies must, again, either invent a story or avoid the prompt altogether. Rather than encourage consultants to think critically about their practices and the decision-making processes that guide them, the Reflection Sheet enlists tutors in self-surveillance. Having failed either to learn the context for writing or to teach the client to proofread and edit, the writing assistant is admonished, however gently, to try harder next time.

Once I had downed a little reflective medicine of my own, I invited tutors to take up the issue of reflective writing over the course of several weekly staff meetings. To break with defensive reasoning, argues Argyris, who studies management consultants, organizations must start at the top. My own example of defensive reasoning served as a catalyst for discussion about reflective thinking in our writing center and the principles and propositions that govern its application. As I mentioned in chapter 2, two more terms from Argyris are again useful here, as they helped to facilitate our analysis of this situation. According to Argyris, we operate via a "theory of action—a set of rules that individuals use to design and implement their own behavior as well as to understand the behavior of others. Usually, these theories of actions become so taken for granted that people don't even realize they are using them." A paradox in human behavior, says Argyris, is that our "espoused" theory of action—the theory we *say* guides our behavior—often contradicts our actual "theory-in-use"—the theory that determines how we *actually* behave (7). Studying examples of their own reflective writing, consultants pointed out that our espoused theory of reflection contradicted our theory-in-use. The stated purpose of the session reflection was to examine tutoring practices and decision-making processes and to share that thinking among writing assistants. In practice, however, reflections tended merely to describe the work done, without a genuine audience beyond the self. Initially, I found this assertion confusing, because reflective writing had long been public, addressed not only to the individual writer, but also to the other tutors who consulted our collection of case histories. Each reflection was filed in duplicate. One copy went into the tutor's file, another in the writer's, so that writing assistants who worked with the same students could be informed about past work, as well as goals for subsequent sessions. Tutors explained, however, that even when they consulted reflections for this purpose, they experienced the writing as a one-way transaction, with the tutor who had written the reflection merely telling them what work was done and what might be addressed in the future. What consultants wanted from reflective writing was dialogue about the theory and practice of tutoring.

Though they chaffed under the burden of composing a session reflection after every tutorial, consultants continued to bring copies of their writing to training meetings, sharing them with the group, using their reflections to prompt lively discussions about a wide array of writing center challenges and questions. When I pointed out their fruitful use of reflection to prompt dialogue, one writing assistant replied, "That's just the point. The reflection isn't on the page. It's in our discussions." He was right. In order to reinvigorate reflective writing, we would need to address these two problems: first, how might reflective writing be made less "I-centered," more dialogic? Second, how might we identify and communicate the genre features that make reflective writing engaging and meaningful to consultants, as writers, readers, and responders? We began with the second problem. Rather than simply tell writing assistants what *I* thought the characteristics of reflective writing are—or should be—I put it to them to determine what features make a "good" reflection. They continued reading our files of reflective writing, with two questions in mind: first, what are the "habits of mind" that characterize engaging reflective writing? Second, what are the rhetorical strategies—or moves—that make reflective writing meaningful to you? Tutors identified the characteristics they thought marked good reflective writing and brainstormed features they did not find in our files, or found infrequently, but which they wanted to see more of. For example, beyond simply describing the work done, a good session reflection might also describe the consultant's decision-making processes. It might describe a specific strategy, offer a rationale for its implementation, and then explore possible alternatives and consequences. Their examination of the characteristics of reflective writing valued in our writing center led us to see that we need to give explicit attention to teaching and learning the genre of reflection.

DESIGNING AN INTERNAL WRITING CENTER
BLOG FOR REFLECTIVE DIALOGUE

Next, we turned to the proposition that, even with some agreed-upon characteristics, "The reflection isn't on the page. It's in our discussions." How could we transform reflective writing from an individual, private enterprise—or worse, a sinister means of surveillance—to a public one in order to enhance learning among tutors? This question prompted us to address another long-standing concern in Chico State's University Writing Center. Old-timers played an important role mentoring novices, but, because of scheduling conflicts, mentors sometimes had limited contact with new tutors. As a remedy, if reflective writing could be posted in an online discussion forum, we speculated, then tutors would have an alternative venue for developing mentoring relationships. In other words, online dialogue might extend reflective writing from *individual* introspection to developing *communal* tutoring practices. To that end, using a hosted weblogging service, we designed a simple online discussion forum where writing assistants could post and comment on their reflective writing. Because several tutors regularly read and write blogs themselves, this setting proved especially appealing, more authentic, to some, than composing in the context of a school assignment. Blogging helped make reflective writing meaningful again.

The screenshot in figure 5.1 shows a typical reflection on the blog. The toolbar down the right margin includes links to the blog's other pages. Posts are divided into two categories: "Question & Answer" and "Weekly Reflections." Also included are links to course materials, resources for tutoring, and popular writing center publications.

A second screenshot (see figure 5.2) includes two comments that writing assistants offered in response to the reflection above. In the right margin is a tag cloud, which highlights major topics of discussion that develop over time. Readers may also find topics of interest by using a keyword search.

Consultants designed the blog based upon their experiences and observations of the needs in our particular writing center. For example, one experienced writing assistant revealed that when he had been a student in the tutor-education course, he often had questions that he was reluctant to ask the director and that he would have liked to have put to a mentor instead. To the online forum for reflective writing, then, tutors added a searchable "Question & Answer" page. Rather than look for *the* answer, during weekly staff meetings, experienced tutors would discuss questions posted to the forum by novices, then take turns offering a range of answers. The purpose would be to explore not only *what* to do in a tutoring session but, more importantly, *why* and *whether*. For example, in answer to the question of whether to read a writer's paper aloud or to ask the writer to read it himself, two mentors brought forward the unconscious theories that guide their contradictory practices. The first acknowledged that her usual practice is to ask the writer to read the paper, or a portion of it, aloud. At the same time, this experienced

Figure 5.1. Sample Blog Post

Figure 5.2. Sample Blog Comments

writing assistant had come to doubt this routine. Writing to a novice led her to reconsider her doubts while justifying her strategy. She explained that she invites writers to read aloud because, among other things, they often self-correct when they read. What's more, she continued, voicing their own writing establishes a productive discourse pattern in the tutoring session, in which the writers do most of the talking. "No, I don't usually do that," challenged another mentor, "because I zone out when I try to listen to someone else read. I usually read aloud, in part because I often work with English language learners, who benefit from hearing what their writing sounds like from a native speaker." When she reads aloud, this consultant is able to take her time, to stop, and to talk about the writing, without feeling that she has interrupted the writer. She went on to explain that controlling the pace of reading also allows her to see patterns of errors and to note them using minimal marking. Although contrary to the previous approach, this, too, seemed like sound reasoning. These two mentors agreed that sometimes when writers read their own work aloud, they do so in what seems like a perfunctory manner, reading the paper in their head rather than the one on paper. Together, they brainstormed advantages and disadvantages of their approaches. Among other strategies, they wondered, what if the client and consultant took turns reading aloud. Our writing center blog, then, isn't merely an online venue for exchanging ideas about tutoring. One purpose is to engage writing center theory through reflective writing. Another purpose, as these two old-timers demonstrate, is to model for novices some habits of mind that characterize reflective thinking, while explicating specific tutoring strategies. In addition to the "Question & Answer" page, then, consultants post weekly reflections and respond to reflections posted by their peers.

Blogging, one tool for developing a reflective community of practice, is well established in writing centers.[3] Melinda Baer (2006), in "Using Weblogs in Your Writing Center," lists a number of benefits. "The most useful aspect of blogs in writing centers," she writes, "is their ability to compile links and discussions (posts) in one place that is accessible anywhere they can get online" (2). In addition to the pragmatic, blogs can be used as a tool for developing thinking.

ANALYSIS OF SAMPLE BLOG POST AND COMMENTS

Below is one example of a reflection posted on our blog and some of the discussion that resulted from it. For readers who wonder if this example is cherry-picked, it is. Not every post and the comments it elicits is as generative as this one. Some posts receive no comments at all. Some exchanges on the blog are shallow and superficial. But many—enough to make this practice worthwhile—are thoughtful, substantive. For the purpose of tutor education, I selected the post and comments examined below because they are illustrative of the features tutors said they valued, features that, for them, exemplify the "habits of mind" that characterize engaging reflective writing. For example, beyond simply describing the work done, the reflection that follows also describes the consultant's decision-making processes. It describes specific strategies and offers reasons for their implementation. Likewise, the responses explore possible alternatives and consequences, sometimes grounding reasons in relevant scholarship.

This excerpt is written by a novice tutor, Esme, who was prompted to write by another student's presentation in class, about a consultation she experienced as a power struggle:

> I had a [first-year composition] student who came in wanting me to "fix" his paper. He had brought his laptop with him, but no printouts of his paper, assignment sheet, or sources. He just wanted me to look at his paper on his laptop and fix it. Heck, we couldn't even both see it properly at the same time because of the sideways resolution. I insisted we print everything out and I graciously allowed him to get on a writing center computer. I made a point that this was a special consideration and that next time he would have to use the computer lab. I also made sure he printed his paper last, so we could go over the assignment sheet before he tried to put the paper under my nose. He kept telling me that he just needed help going over his paper. That he had 3 pages and only needed 2 more. I kept redirecting him to the assignment sheet and asking him questions about his sources and prewriting. Finally, I set down my pen, leaned back in my chair, and just looked at him. After a brief pause, I straight up told him that my job was to help him learn and that I couldn't and wouldn't just fix his paper. After that he seemed to accept that we actually were going to work hard, and everything went very smoothly after that. He left anxious to keep going—he said he was headed to the library–and with an outline in hand. I think he was a little depressed about the amount of work he still had left to do, but he accepted that it was necessary, and he had a plan he could work with.

Esme's frustration here is palpable, but she is proud of both her resolve and her directness. Her refusal to bend to the will of an insistent writer prompted two of her classmates to respond with praise, in part because, like many tutors, they find that resistance, such as Esme's, requires hard-won confidence. Mia responded, "I am so glad that my case presentation was on a topic you could relate to and write about in your post! The next time I have a 'power struggle,' I will follow your example in stepping away from the situation and laying it out straight to the client. It feels good to know other writing assistants are going through the same stuff!" Chris followed with, "Wow! Great examples. In your second session I really liked how much you took the initiative and set the boundaries and put the ball back in his court."

A core principle of a communities-of-practice understanding of learning is that learning is participation, and participation is learning. But participation in what, exactly? Consultants learn to tutor by observing the practices of their peers and by tutoring. But learning by watching and doing tells only part of the story. In their study of apprenticeship as a model of learning, Lave and Wenger (1991) find that rather than novices learning via explicit instruction from masters, "there is very little observable teaching; the more basic phenomenon is learning" (92). Learning, they argue, depends less upon hierarchical master-apprentice relationships than on relations among apprentices: "It seems typical of apprenticeship that apprentices learn mostly in relation with other apprentices" (93). In the writing center, we see old-timers learning from novices as well as novices learning from old-timers. For instance, in the act of answering a new tutor's query about reading a paper aloud, the two responders, both writing assistants for several semesters, are prompted to rethink their practices. But what is the role of expert knowledge in consultants' learning? Lave and Wenger distinguish between a *learning curriculum* and a *teaching curriculum*. "A learning curriculum," they explain, "is a field of learning resources in everyday practice *viewed from the perspective of the learners*" (97; emphasis in original). "Learning" in a community of practice is not something to be acquired. It is *in* the many and varied relationships among community members. By contrast to the open expanse of the learning curriculum, a "teaching curriculum," Lave and Wenger argue, "supplies—and thereby limits—structuring resources for learning" (97).

We should be skeptical, however, of such either/or dichotomous thinking. As designer of the teaching curriculum and a dialogic partner in the community of practice, the writing center director plays an important role on the blog. One function is to socialize consultants into professional conversations about writing center work, to provide critical lenses from which to interpret the work they are undertaking. The blog, then, is not a "pure" student-centered social network. Rather, writing assistants import into their conversations the content, values, assumptions, and beliefs about tutoring that make up the teaching curriculum. In addition to sharing local knowledge generated by their own tutoring experiences, consultants practice the academic moves and ways of talking about tutorials that they learn in the tutoring class as well as other courses they are taking. In this way, the writing center blog becomes a place where tutors rehearse and participate in the community of practice they are entering, engaging, and, indeed, creating. As the following responses to Esme's post illustrate, consultants develop a shared repertoire of resources by engaging the expert knowledge that constitutes the writing center's teaching curriculum. In dialogue, writing assistants explicate expert knowledge. They reflect, incorporate, resist, and revise the teaching curriculum of the tutor-education course. In doing so, they maintain and transform their writing center community of practice as they adopt and adapt its expert knowledge. Likewise, the community sustains and alters individual consultants through their participation.

While praise for Esme may be warranted, a third respondent in this discussion thread complicates our understanding of the power struggle Esme describes by examining the situation through the lens of activity theory, which, as I showed in chapter 3, we use in our writing center as a heuristic for analyzing consultations, and which plays a central role in tutor training. Here is Natalie's response to Esme's post:

> Don't worry about these situations; they arise all of the time. Think about activity theory . . . there must be a distribution of labor in your sessions. If you are doing all of the work, then the student is not learning anything on his or her own. Collaboration is key to working through papers. Furthermore, you cannot feel responsible for not being able to finish the student's paper. If they have a lot of work left to do on it, then they cannot expect to finish in a 45 minute session. I would suggest at the end of the session to persuade them to make another appointment. If their paper is due that day, then tell them to come in earlier next time so they can schedule a few appointments before the due date.

Compare this to the reflection from Yancey's student quoted earlier. There is a fundamental difference between the highly individualized "I-centered" approach to reflection as personal and private, aimed at the self and the surveilling writing center director. By contrast, Natalie's post shows her joining the professional conversation about writing center theory and practice via her local writing center community. She is beginning to think through the analytical framework of activity theory provided by the writing center teaching curriculum. As she demonstrates, knowledge in this writing center community of practice is not generated by consultants in dialogue solely with one another. Rather, Natalie's post draws our attention to the role of the writing center director, who designs and teaches the tutor-education course. I sometimes join in conversations on the blog, but even when I don't participate directly in the conversation, I'm always already present in the exchanges. My knowledge, my course design, my choices of what to read and write about, my values and assumptions about tutor education inform dialogic reflection. Natalie's application of theory reflects a core value I emphasize. In addition to rehearsing—and thus developing—her understanding of the role of the distribution of labor in the activity system of a tutorial, Natalie offers up two alternatives, not in opposition to Esme's resolve but as extensions to it. Natalie is interested in procedural knowledge—what *to do* in a challenging situation like this one. Equally important, she is concerned with the values, assumptions, and beliefs that guide Esme's actions. Why should Esme resist doing the client's work for him?

Following Natalie's post, another writing assistant weighs in, enriching the dialogue by extending Natalie's understanding of activity theory. Michael writes the following:

> I think Natalie's on to something here, in terms of a way to think about this particular power struggle via activity theory. While she mentions the "division of labor" inherent in the activity, as [the activity theorist] David Russell reminds us, "activity systems" are "goal-directed" interactions. [Your] power struggle seems to result because you and the client have different/competing goals in mind.

Like Natalie, Michael makes an academic move, generated, in part, by my participation in our writing center community of practice. In responding to Esme's post, Michael is learning the routines, the ways of talking about writing center work, the intellectual moves I value and promote in tutor training. Naming and quoting from Russell, Michael further identifies with the expert knowledge he has encountered in the tutor-education course. Using activity theory as a heuristic, Michael draws attention to a central question for both writers and tutors: what is the objective—or purpose—for writing? Michael brings to mind a companion refrain in our center: what is the goal—or objective—of the consultation itself? In echoing this refrain, Michael reminds his peers of the necessity, for a successful session, of asking—and answering—these two questions. He goes on to discuss Esme's tutorial in terms of a second framework for analysis—reflective practice—which, like activity theory, is another "espoused" theory in our center:

> Your move, explicitly addressing what you would—and would not—do, helped to break the tension. What's impressive is that you had the presence of mind to stop what you were doing, mid-session, and move differently. That's that "reflection-in-action" we've been talking about in class. (For me, it's usually "reflection inaction." When things aren't going well in a session, I just keep doing what I've been doing, even if it's a complete failure.)
>
> Another way to address this sort of power struggle with the client would be to talk about goals explicitly, in terms of what the student wants to accomplish in the session, and in terms of the writing center's goal to help him learn something he can take with him. (This makes me think back to the "Getting Started" chapter in the ESL collection about the need to negotiate the work that gets done as part of making a plan at the beginning of a session.) Unless we share the same goals, how can the activity system of the session be productive?

This writing consultant engages in double-loop thinking by applying expert knowledge. Referring to reflection-in-action, Michael acknowledges that his 'theory-in-use" does not always meet up with the "espoused theory" of our writing center community of practice. But the goal is not necessarily to bring the two into alignment. Rather, as Michael demonstrates, the purpose of double-loop thinking is to recognize the reasoning we use when we design and implement our actions. Like Natalie before him, Michael uses the blog to articulate his understanding of the principles and propositions that govern practices in our center. He models for Esme the kind of reflective thinking consultants said they value, explaining the "why" of his practice, justifying his strategies by drawing connections to and among multiple texts from the tutor-education course.

To end this thread, another tutor, an old-timer in our center, chimes in. Like Mia and Chris, Carter has high praise for Esme's blunt force. But Carter does not stop there. In her post, she makes a rhetorical move common in double-loop thinking, which writing assistants call "minding the gap," looking for what's missing in the interpretations that precede hers, Carter writes:

> What is interesting about your post, Esme, is your raw truth about the session. And it has provoked such reaction from [writing assistants] that leads them to consider theory. As I've never had the confidence, or rather guts, to stand up directly to a student and stare them down until they crack under pressure and decide to cooperate, I have to applaud your bravery, but at the same time, I question the motivation of the student. Why did [he] come to the writing center? Was he sent here by a professor and did not come under the best of circumstances? What prompted his uncooperative behavior? Was it merely stress, or was there something else going on here?

While Esme locates the source of the session's conflict in the client, Carter suggests another possibility. Her interpretation is prompted by an earlier conversation begun in class, by Yll, a novice tutor who raised the question in a presentation of what assumptions tutors make about clients, and how those beliefs affect the work—for good or ill—in a tutoring session. Carter continues her post this way:

> I'm wondering if it has to do with the client's perceptions of the writing assistant (similar to what Yll was discussing in his case presentation). To what extent was his role determined by perceptions of tutors as students, sorority sisters, pocket-protector geeks, English majors, etc.? Maybe if we try to be clearer about the agenda of work at the beginning of a session, then divisions of labor . . . are not so confrontational to work through in the midst of a session.

With her references back to the importance of setting goals in the activity system of a writing center consultation, Carter, while earlier praising

Esme's confrontational style, concludes by suggesting an altogether different approach. If tutors negotiate the work of a consultation at the outset, perhaps power struggles such as the one Esme describes can be avoided. In this way, Carter recognizes in Esme's response a defensive routine, similar to my earlier defensive reasoning about reflective writing. Unlike the personal, introspective reflections, which bring to mind Romantic notions of the self, this dialogic approach, via the writing center blog, turns reflective writing outward, promoting reciprocal teaching and learning among tutors as they apply the expert knowledge gleaned from the writing center teaching curriculum.

As Baer (2006) cautions about writing center blogs, "You can lead consultants to a blog, but you can't make them post . . . [W]e can provide all the innovative new tools we can think of to facilitate communication and self-motivated learning in our staff, but we will always face users who just won't buy into the new tools we offer" (3–4). In my experience, consultants are more likely to become and remain interested in blogging when it is not just another requirement added to their already busy schedules but when the blog is thoroughly integrated into tutor education, when the writing they do on the blog is frequently and carefully considered in class and in staff meetings, and when blogging is tied to other thinking and writing consultants do. In Esme's case, the learning that resulted, in part, from exchanges on the blog, was demonstrated later in an essay she wrote at the end of the semester:

> Examining my session reflections and responses has made me aware of several things. First, through analyzing my tutoring practices, I realize that not only do I religiously stick to the same routine, but I now better understand *why* sticking to the same routine is not necessarily a good thing. Second, . . . with Grimm and Penti's "Rethinking Agency" [another text from the tutor-education course] in mind, I realize that I have located problems *in students* rather than *in my practices*, particularly for clients who "do not seem to respond readily to conventional teaching or tutoring," or to my preferred routine (195).

Esme's analysis here shows a significant leap in thinking. While Carter wondered if the client's assumptions about Esme had dictated his uncooperative behavior, Esme "minds the gap" further, turning a critical eye upon herself: unlike her initial defensive reasoning, rather than externalizing the problem onto the client, Esme now wonders how the session might have gone differently had she located the tension in herself, in her own—perhaps mistaken—assumptions about the client. In this way, Esme demonstrates, to return to Hillocks (1995) again, the principles of reflective thinking. As Hillocks puts it, "A reflective practitioner will analyze a

new idea in light of its appropriateness to the students and their present knowledge; its fit with available theory, experience, and the goals of
teaching; and its probability for success as judged by the teacher's experience and knowledge" (37). With praise from her peers, Esme has maintained confidence in her ability to challenge a difficult client, with good
results. The discussion of her power struggle is not oversimplified by
binary thinking. Esme's practice is not labeled "wrong," then contrasted
with a "right" way to tutor. Rather, tutors have mined the situation for a
variety—and thus a complexity—of interpretations. In dialogue with her
peers, Esme is led to a productive conclusion about her role as a tutor,
exemplifying double-loop thinking: she may not be able to change the
behavior of a resistant writer, but, with a heightened awareness of her
own values, assumptions, and beliefs, she may be able to change *her* reaction to that behavior. If her earlier post is a fair indication, I would argue
that Esme could not have analyzed her tutoring practices with this depth
of sophistication without the discussion resulting from her initial post.

Importantly, as their blog posts illustrate, when focused explicitly
on reflective thinking, writing center work is not reduced to a set of
how-tos. Rather, the discussion explicates the values, assumptions, and
beliefs, including the principles and propositions supplied by expert
knowledge, which govern tutoring practices. Affording relationships
among experienced and novice writing assistants, dialogic reflection
supports the development of a writing center community of practice.
Discussion threads like the one above draw our attention to the discur-
sive, transactional processes of learning among tutors. While we have
structured tutor education with the notion that old-timers mentor in
newcomers, the distinctions regarding their relative levels of expertise
are not predetermined. As Hsu and Roth (2008) observe in their study
of science lab technicians and high school students, "who is in the know,
who teaches whom, or who has power over someone else is the result
of the processes at hand" (2). In the posts above, for example, experienced consultants, Michael and Carter, prompt Esme, a novice, to consider the necessity of negotiating the agenda of a tutoring session with a
client. At the same time, Esme initiates an opportunity for Michael and
Carter to develop their own understandings of writing center theory
and practice. As a result of his classroom presentation, another novice,
Yll, prompts Carter, an old-timer, to investigate an issue Carter had not
previously considered, the assumptions tutors and writers make about
one another, and the effects those assumptions have on the tutorial.
Their discussion demonstrates that knowledgeability is not constituted
in the individual, in one's head, something mentor consultants impart

to novices, or vice versa. Rather, the online discussion forum exemplifies what Hsu and Roth (2008) call, again, "emergent expertise—knowledgeability that is not a property of individuals but the educational emergence produced during the dual transaction process between participants and mediated by different resources" (8). In other words, as this inquiry into reflective writing illustrates, expertise is not possessed by individuals; rather, it is emergent within their transactions, mediated, not only by resources, such as expert knowledge supplied in the tutor-education course, but also by tools such as the blog. As their posts demonstrate, a communities-of-practice theory of learning brings to the fore the tacit and dynamic aspects of knowledge creation and sharing through dialogue among tutors. Participation in our writing center community is a primary learning event. At the same time, explicit teaching in the tutor-education course is an essential locus of learning. In reflective dialogue—not only among themselves but also through the expert knowledge of its teaching curriculum—consultants develop the shared repertoire essential to a reflective writing center community of practice.

This chapter concludes with an assignment, which invites tutors to reflect on their reflective writing on the blog over time. One goal is to further reinforce the value of reflective thinking by engaging in meta-analysis, looking back to consider what—if any—learning has been afforded by engaging in dialogic reflection on the blog, and with what consequences, not only for oneself, but also for the local writing center community.

ASSIGNMENT: ASSESS YOUR THINKING, WRITING, AND LEARNING ON THE BLOG

After several weeks of contributions to the blog, review your thinking and writing there. Write a brief self-assessment.

First, count your posts and comments: how frequent were your contributions?

Second, pick three to five posts and/or comments, which you think represent your most engaged work. Cut and paste them into a Word doc. Then say, briefly, what makes your contributions engaged—and engaging. Some questions to consider as you evaluate your work (you need not address them all; these are simply options):

- In what ways are your selections typical—or atypical—of your writing on the blog?
- Did you write about an interesting and worthwhile tutoring circumstance?

- In what ways does your writing show a high degree of self-reflection?
- Did you connect your thinking on the blog to class readings and/or discussions?
- In what ways does your writing demonstrate learning on your part?
- In what ways did your posts and comments provoke someone else to think and to write and to learn?
- Does your thinking show any significant change over time?
- In what ways does your writing on the blog demonstrate other positive features not accounted in the questions above?

Overall, what thinking and learning did the blog enable for you, over the course of the semester?

Notes

1. An earlier version of this chapter was previously published in *The Writing Center Journal* 31.1 (2011): 82–105.

2. In the Writing Center at UCF, tutors prefer to be called "peer consultants." In general, throughout this book, I use this name interchangeably with "peer tutor." But in the Writing Center at California State University, Chico, the preferred title was "writing assistant." For that reason, I use "writing assistant" throughout this chapter, as it describes the work of Writing Center staff at Chico State.

3. In addition to *PeerCentered*, a blog for writing consultants and others interested in writing centers to exchange ideas with colleagues from around the world, Jackie Grutsch McKinney has compiled a list of writing center blogs, some public, others internal (Gardner 2008). McKinney's (2009) *Writing Lab Newsletter* column "Geek in the Center: Blogging" elaborates on the uses of blogs in writing centers.

6

PROBLEMS OF PRACTICE: DEVELOPING AN INQUIRY STANCE TOWARD WRITING CENTER WORK[1]

[O]ur notion of inquiry as stance is perspectival and conceptual—a worldview, a critical habit of mind, a dynamic and fluid way of knowing and being in the world of educational practice.

—Marilyn Cochran-Smith and Susan L. Lytle (2009),
Inquiry as Stance: Practitioner Research for the Next Generation

IN THIS CHAPTER

- **Focal Document:** "Problems of Practice Inquiry" assignment
- **Purpose:** to engage tutors in researching questions about writing center work
- **Conceptual Framework for Analysis:** inquiry-based learning
- **Data:** samples of tutor-led inquiry projects and their associated secondary research
- **Assignments:** "Problems of Practice Inquiry" and "Analyzing Commonplace Genres"

In a book whose purpose is to argue for an inquiry-based approach to tutor education, this chapter represents the culmination of that argument, with a focus on a semester-long tutor-led inquiry project. While the chapters that have come before are linked by two primary concerns, a set of conceptual frameworks, which adhere to advance related principles for writing center work, and an inquiry-stance toward writing center work, this chapter digs more deeply into just what an "inquiry stance" entails, including its principles and propositions. In this way, it wraps back around to elaborate on and illustrate the features of inquiry enumerated by Thomas McCann (2014) in the Introduction.

For writing centers that offer a credit-bearing tutor-education course and for those that depend on regular meetings for staff development, sustaining consultants' learning over time can be a challenge. Once tutors complete a course of study, they may feel done, certified to be effective consultants. Staff meetings can easily become preoccupied with practical

DOI: 10.7330/9781607325826.c006

matters, neglecting the writing center as a site of scholarly research and knowledge making. This chapter describes our writing center's approach to ongoing professional development for consultants through the "Problems of Practice Inquiry," an assignment consultants take up each semester, after they have successfully completed the required introductory course. Unlike the course, whose content and organization are determined by the writing center director, this assignment fosters consultants' questions and creates space to pursue agendas important to them. One goal is to develop a *collective inquiry stance* toward writing center research, theory, and practice. Consultants generate questions, collect and interpret relevant resources, then lead discussions about their subjects of inquiry during weekly ongoing tutor-education seminar meetings. In addition to posing questions and gathering and analyzing information, consultants collaborate to propose interventions in our writing center to address the problems they explore. Through an inquiry stance, "learning" is an outcome of "making." As Gordon Wells (2000) puts it in "Dialogic Inquiry in Education: Building on the Legacy of Vygotsky," "Motivated and challenged by real questions, [tutors'] attention is on making answers. Under these conditions, learning is an outcome that occurs because the making requires the student to extend his or her understanding in action—whether the artifact constructed is a material object, an explanatory demonstration, or a theoretical formulation" (61).

The focus of this chapter are the activities that take place around the "Problems of Practice" assignment, below.

Assignment: Problems of Practice Inquiry

This semester, in addition to peer tutoring in the writing center, you will take up some important question or problem to research, and then lead us during a weekly seminar meeting in discussion of various ways to address that concern. Our goal is to inquire collaboratively into issues that arise from your writing center work by examining research and conversations in the field about writing center theory and practice. Together, you will learn to look more deeply into important matters of teaching and learning in the writing center for a more reflective, dynamic tutoring experience as a result. If this inquiry works well, it will enhance the process and content of your ongoing professional development as a writing consultant. It will add understanding and capacity to your practice. It will also generate innovation in our writing center community of practice.

Some steps to get you started:

- Identify a specific question, problem, dilemma, or issue related to your work in the writing center to investigate this semester. You may work on an individual project, but you are encouraged, instead, to work together with one or two of your colleagues. You'll learn more and have a richer experience talking over and researching your inquiry jointly.

- Discuss your inquiry with staff at other writing centers. Join the WCenter discussion forum. To subscribe, contact Elizabeth Bowen <elizabeth.bowen@ttu.edu>. To view the archives, go to <http://lyris .ttu.edu/read/?forum=wcenter>. To post a message, address your e-mail to the following: <wcenter@lyris.ttu.edu>. You may also join the conversation about writing center work on the *PeerCentered* blog at <http://www.peercentered.org/>.

- Use databases such as the Education Resource Information Center (ERIC) <http://www.eric.ed.gov/> to learn what writing center specialists have written about your subject. Try the UCF Hitt Library "Education Full Text" database too: <http://library.ucf.edu/>.

- Read three to four relevant journal articles or book chapters that address your question. Together, these should give you a sense of some varied viewpoints that make up the conversation in the field. See especially *The Writing Lab Newsletter* at <https://wlnjournal.org/> and *The Writing Center Journal* at <http://writingcenterjournal.org/>. Both have online archives. Look, too, at the online journal *Praxis: A Writing Center Journal*: <http://www.praxisuwc.com/>. *The Dangling Modifier* at <http://sites.psu.edu/thedanglingmodifier/> is another useful source for writing center scholarship. Journals such as *College Composition and Communication* and *College English* also host writing center research.

- Talk with the writing center director and assistant director beforehand about your inquiry question and, later, your ideas for leading discussion of your question during a seminar meeting. We'll help you formulate your inquiry, research it, and make a plan for facilitating talk about it.

- Choose a date to lead discussion about your inquiry. First, sum up what you've learned. Consider making a brief handout. Do more than talk at us. You may pick a short selection or excerpt from your research for us to read together. You may plan an engaging activity for us to do. Your role as discussion leader is to involve us in joint problem solving, in thinking about ways to apply what you've learned to change in our writing center. The goal is to generate ideas about what intentional actions we might take to address the question you've researched.

- Add copies of your selected reading and other resources you gather or create to our collection on our Canvas Webcourse. We'll put hard copies in a binder for circulation in the Writing Center. We'll also consider if your materials may be suited to a page on our web site and/or the Writing Center's internal blog.

* * *

An "inquiry stance," as Marilyn Cochran-Smith and Susan Lytle suggest in the epigraph that opens this chapter, is a "critical habit of mind" Cochran-Smith and Lytle (2009). It prompts tutors to see writing center work as we view scholarly disciplines, not merely as something one does, a set of instrumental strategies or tasks, but as a field of study, of research and knowledge making. Like many writing centers, central to our community of practice is the belief that, while consultants need procedural knowledge in order to work effectively, a set of how-tos is insufficient. Tutor education, then, encourages an inquiry stance, which involves ongoing questioning, asking why and whether, wondering, researching, generating alternatives, testing, reviewing, and revising options. Importantly, the purpose of inquiry is not simply to solve problems or to correct flawed practice. Its aim is to examine both what we do and the rules and reasoning—the habits of mind—that govern what we do. From an inquiry stance, then, the role of consultants is not only to tutor writing. It is to participate in ongoing learning and knowledge making. As Cochran-Smith and Lytle (2009) put it, "[P]ractitioners are deliberative intellectuals who constantly theorize practice as part of practice itself and . . . the goal of teacher learning initiatives is the joint construction of local knowledge, the questioning of common assumptions, and thoughtful critique of the usefulness of research generated by others both inside and outside contexts of practice" (2). Multiple processes are involved in an inquiry stance. Three are described in the analysis follows: question posing, collaborative conversation among peers, and purposeful use of a variety of resources (Whitin 2007, 20).

QUESTION POSING

The key to a good "Problems of Practice Inquiry" is a researchable question, which engages both the individual consultant and the local writing center community. A good question is one that practitioners and specialists have wondered about and discussed, perhaps in writing center scholarship, perhaps in other disciplines. A good question is also open-ended, allowing for a wide range of alternative, sometimes contradictory, answers. But a consultant need not begin with a clearly formulated question. In fact, some of the best questions emerge only after preliminary research, or in pursuit of some other inquiry altogether. Questions may concern tutoring directly: "Should tutors take a more directive or nondirective approach, or some combination of the two?" Questions may address broader issues: "What should be the place of a writing center within an institution—in an English department, a learning center, as an independent program—and with what consequences?" Whatever the inquiry, question posing begins with genuine local concerns. Consultants encounter challenges and wonder how to address them. They are curious about writing center structures, decision-making, and the conceptual frameworks that support them. In our experience, formulating a researchable question is no easy task. Consultants first need time to work in the writing center and to engage in close, sustained observation. They need guided practice framing questions and pursuing answers, sometimes to frustrating dead ends. With these challenges in mind, we introduce the "Problems of Practice" assignment early in the tutor-education course, long before consultants begin their own inquiry projects. Throughout the semester, we draw attention to possible areas of inquiry and consider relevant resources. For example, in his third week as a novice consultant, Jackson described a tutoring session in which he had worked with a student who was writing a paper about dyslexia. Kyndra, the writer, explained that she had recently discovered that dyslexia was the cause, since childhood, of her reading and writing difficulties. In her paper, she explored what she had learned as a result of studying this learning disability. A second peer consultant, Haley, had also worked with Kyndra. During their consultation, Kyndra told Haley of her desire to use her newfound knowledge to inform others about dyslexia and to advocate for students with learning differences. Haley suggested we invite Kyndra to a Writing Center staff meeting to tell consultants about dyslexia, to answer questions, and to explore strategies tutors might use to better support writers like her. This staff meeting led us to read Julie Neff's (1994) chapter "Learning Disabilities and the Writing Center." We turned also to *The Writing Center Resource Manual* for additional reading (Silk 2002, 4.1). We consulted local resources, too, such as an expert in our campus office of Student Accessibility Services. Repeated modeling of question posing and resource gathering like this helps to engender inquiry as a collective habit of mind in our writing center.

Posing questions about writing center research, theory, and practice takes multiple forms and satisfies various purposes, depending upon the peer consultant. In a previous writing center I directed, most graduate students in the tutor-education course there did not enroll voluntarily. Rather, as new teaching assistants in English, they were required to complete the course and to tutor for twenty hours each week to fulfill the first-year requirement of their graduate assistantship. Some graduate assistants, whose primary interest was in literature or creative writing, came to the writing center with reluctance, with little prior knowledge of or interest in rhetoric and composition or writing center work in particular. The "Problems of Practice Inquiry" positioned them, nevertheless, as curious scholars, observing writing center work closely, wondering about it, raising questions, and pursuing answers. This assignment introduced tutors to a wide range of resources outside of literary studies, including experts and texts in rhetoric, composition, literacy studies, education, communication, and beyond. It provided opportunities to learn the discourses and genres that mediate knowledge making in these disciplines. As novice graduate students professionalizing in English studies, they gained valuable experience searching for, reading, interpreting, writing about, and leading discussions on scholarly research beyond their primary areas of interest.

While most graduate consultants work in our center for only a year before moving on to teach first-year composition, undergraduate consultants may return for multiple semesters after completing the tutor-education course. For these tutors, many from disciplines other than English, the "Problems of Practice Inquiry" extends and develops their knowledge of and participation in the field of writing center studies. Sometimes intimidated by their graduate peers, as undergraduate consultants become deeply immersed in a question, they gain a sense of agency and power by making their enthusiasm and developing expertise public. Long-time professional staff, too, benefit from raising questions about writing center work. Through the "Problems of Practice Inquiry," veterans, who sometimes slip into an instrumental view of tutoring as merely a set of routines they do, may be prompted to more reflective practice. They may be enlivened by new ideas or forgotten professional conversations about tutoring. With a long view of a writing center's history and operation, veterans may take up important questions they see have been neglected over time, prompting needed change. "Working from and with an inquiry stance," as Cochran-Smith and Lytle (2009) suggest, "involves a continual process of making current arrangements problematic; questioning the ways knowledge and practice are constructed, evaluated, and used, and assuming that part of the work of practitioners individually and collectively is to participate in educational and social change" (121).

COLLABORATIVE CONVERSATIONS

Central to an inquiry stance is collaboration. "In its simplest terms," write Alexandra Weinbaum et al. (2004),

> collaborative inquiry is the process by which colleagues gather in groups to pursue, over time, the questions about teaching and learning that the group members identify as important. Groups develop their understanding of an issue through framing a question, identifying artifacts or "evidence" that help respond to it, sharing perspectives on the evidence, reflecting on the partial or provisional answers that emerge, and revising the question in light of experiences and discussion. (2–3)

Through collaborative inquiry, consultants observe the work of the writing center, make sense of their experiences, learn from the perspectives of one another, and draw upon resources remote and local to enhance tutoring and learning in the center. Because collaborative learning is not necessarily reinforced outside the writing center, tutors may sometimes see it as valuable for tutees, but not central to their own learning. The "Problems of Practice Inquiry" illustrates a central principle of writing center work: that knowledge is situated in social activity (Lave and Wenger 1991). Participation in genuine inquiry as a group activity can transform both the individual and the writing center community of practice as a whole. As co-participants in a community of inquiry, consultants become involved emotionally, socially, and cognitively. Together they co-construct their knowledge in a social context. Good questions, which allow for alternative possibilities, encourage tutors to collaborate with one another in order to make shared understandings. The same questions also prompt consultants to negotiate dissensus, to accept sometimes-uneasy disagreements, both theoretical and practical, among themselves and with experts. While inquiry groups have become commonplace in professional development for teachers, this assignment elevates inquiry to a prominent place in writing center tutor education. An inquiry stance promotes reflective practice, involving tutors not only individually but also as a community of practice (Smith 2005). As Michele Crockett (2002) points out in "Inquiry as Professional Development: Creating Dilemmas Through Teachers' Work," "the dominant approach to teacher development locates reflective actions within individuals rather than within communities" (609). A collaborative inquiry stance, however, Cochran-Smith and Lytle (2009) caution, "should not be equated simply with being reflective or with developing an open and questioning intellectual viewpoint about practice; these are necessary, but not sufficient aspects of an inquiry stance" (121). When consultants work from a genuine inquiry stance, every aspect of a writing center becomes subject to questioning. Central to an inquiry stance, then, is not just figuring out how to get tutoring done, but, more importantly, as Cochran-Smith and Lytle put it, "[I]t is social and political in the sense of deliberating about what gets done, why to get it done, who decides, and whose interests are served" (121).

For example, in another "Problems of Practice Inquiry," Ezra and Tia questioned how writing centers are assessed. They began by wondering if students' papers were better after tutoring sessions than before. Together they read widely in the field about the challenges inherent in writing center assessment. They followed conversations on the *WCenter* discussion forum about formulating learning outcomes for writing centers (Cain 2010). They examined assessment plans from other writing centers, considering outcomes statements and both direct and indirect measures. While they could see the value of formulating outcomes, Ezra and Tia also wondered about the confines of such statements, taking up Wells's (2000) observation that outcomes may be both "aimed for" and "emergent." As he points out, "Outcomes of activity cannot be completely known or prescribed in advance; while there may be prior agreement about the goal to be aimed for, the route that is taken depends upon emergent properties of the situation—the problems encountered and the human and material resources available for making solutions" (58). An effective writing center assessment, then, would need to be flexible enough to see, document, and value unanticipated outcomes. Even with a narrow focus on tutees' writing, with so many variables to consider, making meaningful judgments about improvements in individual papers quickly proved more vexing than Ezra and Tia had at first imagined. During the course of their inquiry, these two consultants learned, among other things, that writing centers have become increasingly interested in not only the impact of our services on writers and their writing but also on tutors themselves. Ezra and Tia became particularly interested in *The Peer Writing Tutor Alumni Research Project*, developed by Harvey Kail, Paula Gillespie, and Brad Hughes (Hughes, Gillespie, and Kail 2010). Their survey attempts to learn how significant the experience of collaborative learning is for peer tutors after they graduate from college. Questions ask what former consultants have taken with them from their training and experience as writing tutors. In addition to prompting our writing center to reconsider its own assessment plan, outcomes, and measures, *The Peer Writing Tutor Alumni Research Project* led Ezra and Tia to reconsider why we might conduct an assessment in the first place, whose interests might be served, and what an assessment design reveals about a writing center's underlying values, assumptions, and beliefs, indeed, its very mission. By valuing not merely improved papers or better writers but also the long-term growth and development of tutors themselves, *The Peer Writing Tutor Alumni Research Project* led these two consultants to see and to value their own experiences as an important measure of our writing center's effectiveness.

The "Problems of Practice Inquiry" promotes collaborative discussion within a writing center, while introducing consultants to professional conversations in the field, both published and informal, via sites such as the *WCenter* discussion forum and the *PeerCentered* blog. In "Beyond the House of Lore: WCenter as Research Site" Paula Gillespie (2002) argues that "WCenter goes well beyond lore and tries to look at cause-effect relationships and theories that underlie our various and/or canonical practices. WCenter allows knowledge to be made by a community in a collaborative way" (50). This assignment invites tutors, particularly novice consultants, to join in the professional conversation, to participate in *inquiry*, as Gillespie defines it, as "a form of research more likely to lead to scholarship or empirical research or to serve as an invention heuristic for such study" (42).

This inquiry project also encourages cross- and inter-institutional cooperation. For example, in another "Problems of Practice Inquiry" completed at the University of North Carolina at Charlotte Writing Resources Center, consultants began with observation over time of online tutoring in our writing center. David immersed himself in recent research, curious not only about the variety of available technologies but also their underlying assumptions about teaching, learning, and writing pedagogy. He investigated online tutoring at other writing centers. As a result of his inquiry, we abandoned e-mail consultations and embarked on a collaboration with our campus Center for Teaching and Learning to pilot a new method of online tutoring, using a web-based platform of synchronous chat, live audio and video, and document and application sharing. David's insights, although impressive, were not singularly his own. They were products of ongoing social activity and distributed cognition, both within and beyond our writing center. David spent a summer designing user documents for both consultants and tutees, along with a web page of related resources. Almost as soon as we launched the pilot, however, we learned that several tutors, less comfortable with the new technology than David, found the platform clunky and off-putting. Later, as a writing center alumnus himself, David enrolled in a graduate seminar on digital documentation, where he explored a new, more user-friendly web-based technology for online tutoring. What began as an inquiry in the writing center persisted as a subject of interest for David, which led to a primary research project on online tutoring and further graduate study. Developing an inquiry stance, then, is not aimed merely at problem solving. Rather, its goal is to be open to wonder, puzzlement, partial or provisional answers, and continuing exploration.

RESOURCES

Consultants use multiple resources in the "Problems of Practice Inquiry" to confirm and to complicate their observations of local practice and to generate ideas about intentional actions we might take in our writing center to address the questions they research. Carter's inquiry into reading is a good example. She began by noticing that she frequently worked with clients not only on their writing but also on reading challenging academic texts. What, she wondered, do consultants do to support reading practices in the writing center? And how might we enhance tutor education to give more attention to reading pedagogy? As a novice undergraduate consultant, Carter was initially hesitant about her ability to be an effective tutor. Surrounded by confident graduate consultants, Carter doubted her readiness to tutor writing and even considered dropping the tutor-education course. An English education major, Carter was preparing to become a teacher, so she stuck with tutoring, persuaded that the experience would serve her well in the future. Her "Problems of Practice Inquiry" helped to develop not only Carter's knowledge of reading research and pedagogy, but, equally important, her confidence as a writing consultant and future teacher. In a reflection about her inquiry, Carter wrote the following:

> Thinking of potential questions I had regarding writing center practice, I was not really sure in which direction I wanted to go. During much of the fall semester, training and tutoring felt overwhelming to me. As one of only two undergraduates in the tutor-training course, initially I felt that I was not qualified to do the work that was asked of me. I began to doubt myself as well as my future plans to become a high school English teacher. Much of what I struggled with during the fall seemed to calm as the spring semester approached. I wanted to accomplish, in my second semester working in the writing center, a way to connect my new experiences and training to my developing knowledge of teaching writing and reading.
>
> I began to think through aspects of training, not only as a writing center tutor, but also as a future teacher. Since tutoring and teaching have much in common, I figured that I would develop as a teacher and potentially help my future students if I could make meaningful connections between resources of the two. In teacher training, I have been taught the importance of reading, reading comprehension, the practices of proficient readers, and how these contribute to becoming a good writer. With all this going through my mind, I decided that I needed a way to relate the theory and practice of reading instruction, which I had been studying in one of my education classes, to the theory and practice of teaching writing.
>
> My "Problems of Practice Inquiry" blossomed. Questioning how reading research and theory relates and, in turn, plays an important role in the writing center, I became deeply interested in ways to connect reading and writing pedagogy, not only in the writing center, but also in preparation for my teaching career.

As Carter's experience suggests, the "Problems of Practice Inquiry" is not only about learning to research, think about, and do writing center work. It's about identity-making. As Wells (2000) puts it, "who a person becomes depends critically on which activity systems he or she participates in and on the support and assistance he or she receives from other members of the relevant communities in appropriating the specific values, knowledge, and skills that are enacted in participation" (54). Just as question posing requires support and repeated modeling, so gathering and mining available resources also depends on deliberate affordances. With little knowledge of reading theory and pedagogy, myself, I took the role of co-inquirer with Carter, encouraging her to begin with her own experience and knowledge of reading.

With space to pursue an agenda important to her, Carter observed and asked questions about her reading pedagogy and that of her writing center colleagues. She examined her prior knowledge and consulted new resources from her course on reading theory and pedagogy. She sought answers from writing center scholarship. She prompted further learning about reading in our writing center, including consultation with a reading specialist, and revision to the tutor-education course syllabus to give explicit attention to teaching reading in a writing center context. Later, while leading discussion about her inquiry during a weekly meeting, Carter offered up strategies, such as "questioning the author," to use in reading consultations in the writing center:

- What is the author trying to say?
- What is the author's message?
- What is the author talking about?
- That's what the author says, but what does it mean?
- How does that connect with what the author already told us?
- How does that fit in with what the author already told us?
- What information has the author added here that connects or fits in with _____?
- Does that make sense?
- Is that said in a clear way?
- Did the author explain that clearly? Why or why not? What's missing? What do we need to figure out or find out?
- Did the author tell us that?
- Did the author give us the answer to that? (Beck et al. 1996, 389–90)

Carter also looked to writing center research for information about teaching reading, including W. Gary Griswold's (2006) "Postsecondary Reading: What Writing Center Tutors Need to Know." Griswold's research confirmed Carter's felt sense that, though writing center training texts remind us of the importance of reading, few explain what, specifically, consultants might do to develop tutees' reading practices. Griswold recommends that consultants learn not only specific strategies for supporting reading development but also the theory that justifies and explains those pedagogical activities. While Carter and her peers found a list of strategies, such as "questioning the author" comforting, Griswold complicated their thinking, introducing the idea that different kinds of texts require different reading strategies, and thus different pedagogical interventions, such as mapping and annotation. From another of her texts from her education course, Carter learned other strategies used by proficient readers:

> *Predict*: Based on what happened in this section, what are your predictions for the next section?
>
> *Question*: What questions do you have? Consider questions that have answers "right there" in the text, questions that require "thinking and searching," or questions that require your "opinion" to answer.
>
> *Clarify*: What words, ideas, or parts of the text are clear to you?
>
> *Summarize*: Implement a process to arrive at a clear and concise summary. (Fisher and Frey 2004, 159)

A second consultant, Simon, picked up Carter's inquiry into reading to extend our thinking further. Immediately, we hit a dead end. A query to the blog *PeerCentered* yielded no response. But a question to the *WCenter* discussion forum reminded us to investigate local knowledge in addition to scholarly sources. On the forum, one respondent recommended:

> I'd start . . . with your tutors. Ask them what reading strategies they employ when they get stuck. They probably know the answers you seek but haven't thought about themselves (yet) as "experts" in reading for writing (or writing for reading comprehension). But they know what kinds of thoughts pop into their heads when they get lost or encounter a text that is unlike others they've read . . . And they probably know . . . how they muddle through. You can have them bring in texts that . . . give them trouble and use them to model the breakdowns and strategies.
>
> . . . [I]f you have a diverse group of tutors, chances are you'll have a variety of challenges and strategies from which to learn. (Fels 2010)

Discussing their own wide variety of reading strategies, consultants began to view tidy lists like those commonly found in Carter's reading textbooks with some skepticism, considering both their strengths and weaknesses. On the one hand, they provide good ideas, many of which are confirmed by tutors' experiences as readers themselves. On the other, if applied too prescriptively, strategies may foster a rigid, mechanical approach to reading pedagogy. A third consultant, Anna, interested in writing development among students with learning disabilities, posted several videos, excerpts from Richard Lavoie's (1989) *How Difficult Can This Be? The F.A.T City Workshop—Understanding Learning Disabilities*, on our writing center blog. These served as the basis for discussion in another meeting. In particular, a segment about reading comprehension through vocabulary helped consultants to understand that, no matter what the reader's abilities, a bottom-up, skill-and-drill approach to learning vocabulary, for instance, is ineffective for improving reading. Proficient reading requires much more than understanding the words. Readers need background knowledge. They need to understand the context for the words.

GOING PUBLIC

The culmination of the "Problems of Practice Inquiry" is for peer tutors to go public, to share what they've learned with the wider writing center community of practice. To go public with their inquiry into reading, which extended the related projects of several colleagues, Anna and Gabriel produced the following document to share. They also led a reading comprehension activity, described below, taken from Stephanie Harvey and Harvey Daniels (Harvey and Daniels 2009).

"PROBLEMS OF PRACTICE" SAMPLE: INQUIRY INTO TUTORING READING

Problem: Many students who visit the Writing Center need help not with writing but with reading. Because much of the writing students do in college requires them to respond to something they've read, the writing can be impossible to do when the reading isn't clear.

Inquiry Question: What can peer consultants do to assist tutees to read and understand challenging academic texts?

Activity[2]:

Part 1: Read the following passage until you feel you understand it well.

MS2 Phage Coat Protein - RNA Interaction

This system is being studied for **three reasons**: (1) it is an example of a sequence-specific RNA-protein interaction, (2) it participates in a **well-behaved** in vitro capsid assembly reaction, and (3) it is a good model system to study how protein finds a target on a large RNA molecule. Available are an X-ray crystal structure of the RNA-protein complex and an NMR structure of the free RNA hairpin target. Current efforts focus on understanding how the **thermodynamic** details of sequence-specific "recognition" is achieved. We have made mutations in all the amino acids believed to make contact with the RNA and are evaluating the affinity of the mutant proteins to the normal RNA target as well as to targets that have single atom changes in either the bases or the phosphodiester backbone. It is already clear that nearly all the contacts predicted by the co-crystal structure contribute to the total free energy of binding. Thus, unlike several protein-protein interfaces that have been analyzed in a similar way, there are **no "hot spots"** that dominate the affinity. However, we have several examples where affinity and specificity are defined by structural elements of the RNA in its **free form.**

—Olke C. Uhlenbeck, PhD, Professor of Molecular Biosciences

Part 2: Reading Comprehension Quiz:

1. How many reasons are there for studying this system?

2. What is the nature of the in vitro capsid assembly reaction?

3. Current research focuses on what details of sequence-specific recognition?

4. How many "hot spots" dominate the affinity?

5. In what form are there examples of RNA where affinity and specificity are defined by structural elements?

Part 3: Reflection and Discussion:

Try to remember exactly what was going on inside your head as you attempted to make meaning of this short passage: what kinds of thinking did you use to make sense of it? Talk with a partner about your strategies.

Some Recommended Reading Research

- Beck, Isabel L., Margaret G. McKeown, Cheryl Sandora, and Linda Kucan. "Questioning the Author: A Yearlong Classroom Implementation to Engage Students with Text." *Elementary School Journal* 96.4 (1996): 385–414.

- Harvey, Stephanie, and Harvey Daniels. *Comprehension and Collaboration: Inquiry Circles in Action.* Portsmouth, NH: Heinemann, 2009.

- Griswold, W. Gary. "Postsecondary Reading: What Writing Center Tutors Need to Know." *Journal of College Reading and Learning* 37.1 (Fall 2006): 61–72.

- Lavoie, Richard. *How Difficult Can This Be? The F.A.T. City Workshop— Understanding Learning Disabilities.* Films Media Group, 1989. Films on Demand. 8 Oct. 2010.

- Tierney, Robert J., and P. David Pearson. "Toward a Composing Model of Reading." *Language Arts* 60 (1993): 568–80.

What Does the Research Show?

Proficient adult readers don't just randomly flail about when our comprehension breaks down. Instead, they deploy a very specific repertoire of thinking strategies that we have developed over years of experience. What are some of those strategies?

- Monitor comprehension (notice when the text makes sense and when it doesn't).
- Activate and connect to background knowledge (learn about the subject; most "reading difficulties" are actually "prior knowledge" problems).
- Ask questions (wonder about concepts, outcomes, genre).
- Infer and visualize meaning (merge background knowledge with clues in the text).
- Determine importance (determine what the author wants the reader to take away).
- Synthesize and summarize (use parts to see the whole—read for the gist)

What Can Peer Writing Consultants Do to Facilitate Reading?

First, remember that different kinds of texts call for different kinds of reading strategies. Start by determining what kind of text it is and what the reader intends to do with it. In other words, what's the purpose for reading? Next, model strategies you use to make sense of difficult texts; create opportunities for readers to practice those strategies. Finally, keep in mind the three principles from reading research:

1. Reading principle: The more you read, the better you will read.
2. Response principle: Reading comprehension requires that learners have opportunities to talk, write, and draw about their thinking.
3. Explicit instruction principle: Readers need direct instruction in strategies to decode and comprehend challenging texts.

* * *

As this example illustrates, through multiple, overlapping, intersecting tutor inquiries, and a wide range of resources, consultants built one inquiry on another and, in the process, developed a deeper understanding of tutoring reading. Different texts read for different purposes require different strategies. All texts are embedded in specific social practices related to specific social identities. With this expansion of knowledge, consultants reconsidered their roles as reading facilitators. Insights from these inquiry projects led consultants to see that rather than simply apply a set of reading strategies, consultants need to work together with readers to understand the particular social practices and identities that structure complex academic texts. Together with readers, consultants need to explore questions of genre when coaching reading: what is the work of the text? What is it doing? What identity does it assume of the reader? To put it another way, what ways of seeing, thinking, being, and doing in the world does the text engage and invite? Multiple inquiries into reading also led consultants to insist on further study of reading, including explicit attention to reading in the tutor-education course. As students of writing, they found Robert J. Tierney and P. David Pearson's treatment of reading particularly appealing. In "Toward a Composing a Model of Reading," the authors argue that reading is like writing, an act of composing, involving "planning," "drafting," "aligning," "revising," and "monitoring" (Tierney and Pearson 1993, 568–78). Emphasizing reading as not merely a receptive activity but a productive one, Tierney and Pearson prompted consultants to consider the ways facilitating reading mirrors facilitating composing in a writing center.

After implementing the "Problems of Practice Inquiry" in two different writing centers, over multiple semesters, I've seen a myriad of hoped-for and unexpected outcomes. Because projects reflect the interests of tutors themselves, peer consultants become knowledgeable, and, thus, empowered to speak and act on subjects of importance to them. As a result, they press for action in response to their inquiry projects. This leads, again and again, to positive change in our writing center. For example, two graduate consultants, Landon and Brandy, who investigated the intersection of technology uses and space design were led to advocate for a turn in our writing center toward a "multiliteracy center" (Sheridan and Inman 2010). Because their inquiry project met with such enthusiasm, these two PhD students then wrote a proposal to redesign an area of our writing center to include new technologies to support work on digital and, in particular, multimodal composing and responding. Following this renovation, Landon and Brandy designed a qualitative research study to examine interactions in this new space. Later, they published their findings (Berry and Dieterle 2016). Other inquiry projects, too, have prompted both primary research and significant changes in our writing center. One semester, for instance, multiple inquiry projects circled around questions about Wardle and Downs's (2014) *Writing about Writing* curriculum in our first-year composition program. Some tutors had been through this curriculum themselves, while others were unfamiliar. Inquiry projects led us to design an entire semester's tutor-education curriculum to focus on *Writing about Writing*, so that tutors could become better informed and more helpful to the large number of first-year writing students who visit our writing center for assistance. Similarly, with several inquiry projects taking up questions about how best to support multilingual writers, in response we designed a semester-long curriculum for experienced tutors to dig more deeply into the research, theory, and practice of tutoring multilingual writers. This initiative coincided with the creation on our campus of a new "Global Achievement Academy," whose aim is to recruit, retain, and support a growing number of international students. Those students, many of them multilingual writers, would soon be enrolled in first-year composition and would find their way to the University Writing Center. With a history of strong support for multilingual writers in our writing center, tutors were eager to learn more to prepare for the changing demographics of student writers on our campus.

In another instance, a series of inquiry projects concerning questions about tutoring in unfamiliar disciplines led us to design a semester of inquiry into commonplace genres in the university. In an informal conversation with Brad Hughes at the 2014 IWCA conference, two peer tutors in our writing center mentioned their interest in genre-based pedagogy. Hughes speculated that there are only ten to twelve commonplace genres in the university, and so if tutors could become knowledgeable about them, then they might be better prepared to assist writers in learning them. We found Hughes's speculation both provocative and tantalizing. We returned to our writing center, wondering what some of the most frequent genres might be, and so we surveyed tutors about their experiences, asking not only about commonplace genres they encountered as tutors but also about those they had learned about as writers themselves and unfamiliar genres they wanted to learn more about. With widespread interest among tutors in learning more about genre, we developed the more narrowly focused inquiry assignment below, adapted from Anis Bawarshi and Mary Jo Reiff's "Rhetorical Genre Studies" in *Genre: An Introduction to History, Theory, Research, and Pedagogy* (Bawarshi and Reiff 2010).

ASSIGNMENT: ANALYZING COMMONPLACE GENRES

Purpose

One challenge of tutoring in a writing center is that you routinely meet writers from unfamiliar disciplines, writing in genres whose rules and conventions may be unknown to you. But if you lead with ignorance, confiding, "I've never written a lab report; what does it look like?" then the writer may lose confidence in you.

To address this challenge, this semester we'll study the concept of "genres." According to Michael Carter, Carolyn Miller, and Ann Penrose, "understanding a genre involves understanding the nexus of audience, purpose, convention, and text within that social situation" (Carter, Miller, and Penrose 1998, 3). Research suggests that explicit teaching about genre can help writers negotiate the variety of genres they encounter. As Irene Clark (1999) points out, "attention to genre has particularly important implications for assisting the marginalized student populations that writing centers are so well-suited to help and, in fact, for whom they were originally instituted" (14). While becoming an expert in every genre is impossible, tutors *can* begin to understand how genres help members of communities do the work of that community.

To that end, you'll work in a small group this semester to collect samples of common genres often seen in the writing center, analyze them, teach other tutors about the genre you analyzed, and then design informational resources about them, which we can then use as teaching tools for both peer consultants and writers. The big questions you'll explore are the following:

- What *community* or *communities* use this genre?
- What *work* does the genre do within that community?
- What *patterns* are apparent across multiple examples of the genre?
- What is the *significance* of these patterns within the community that uses this genre?
- How will this *genre knowledge* help you tutor effectively in the Writing Center?

Required Reading

To ground your learning about genre, we'll do some reading together:

- Clark, Irene. "Addressing Genre in the Writing Center." *Writing Center Journal* 20.1 (1999): 7–32.
- Dean, Deborah. *Genre Theory: Teaching, Writing, and Being.* Urbana, IL: NCTE, 2008. 3–41, 46–49, and 55–61.
- Dinitz, Sue, and Susanmarie Harrington. "The Role of Disciplinary Expertise in Shaping Writing Tutorials." *Writing Center Journal* 33.2 (2014): 73–98.

To Do

1. *Form a small group* of no more than three.
2. *Select* one of the genres listed below to study.

3. *Collect* at least three authentic *samples* of the genre, including samples from one specific community and similar uses of that genre in other communities. For example, you might choose the genre of the annotated bibliography, then collect samples of annotated bibliographies from several communities that use that genre. You might collect samples from first-year composition courses and from health sciences research courses and from education courses. A useful sample is typical or representative of the genre, not an idiosyncratic outlier. We're looking for effective examples we can use as models in the Writing Center. Start by asking faculty who teach in disciplines that use the genre if they have samples they are willing to share. Gather copies of related assignments or prompts as well. Also look for examples in textbooks and manuals about the genre. You may also contact professionals outside the university for sample documents.

4. Look at the samples and *describe the situation and work* of the genre:

   a. *Context:* Where does the genre appear? In what discipline, for example?

   b. *Subject:* What problem, issues, or questions does the genre address?

   c. *Work of the genre:* Why do writers write this genre and why do readers read it? What purposes does the genre fulfill?

   d. *Participants:* Who uses the genre? *Writers:* Who writes in the genre? What characteristics/special knowledge must writers of this genre possess? Under what circumstances do writers produce the genre? *Readers:* Who reads texts in this genre? What characteristics/special knowledge must readers of this genre possess? Under what circumstances do readers encounter the genre?

5. Working from the samples you've collected, identify and describe the *recurrent features of structure and language* in the genre:

   a. What *content* is typically included? What is excluded? How is the content treated? What sorts of examples and illustrations are used? What counts as evidence?

   b. What *rhetorical appeals* are used? What appeals to logos, ethos, pathos appear?

   c. How are texts in the genre *structured?* What are their parts and how are they *organized?*

   d. In what *format* are texts of this genre presented? What layout or appearance is common? How long is a typical text in this genre?

   e. What types of *sentences* do texts in the genre typically use? How long are they? Are they simple or complex, passive or active? Are the sentences varied? Do they share a certain style?

   f. What *diction* (types of words) is most common? Is jargon used? Is the language formal or informal?

6. Now *analyze* why these patterns are *significant* to the community that uses them: what *values, assumptions, beliefs, and goals* are revealed through your analysis? Consider the following:

   - What do participants have to know or believe to understand or appreciate the genre?
   - Who is invited into the genre, and who is excluded?
   - What roles for writers and readers does the genre encourage or discourage?
   - How is the subject of the genre treated?
   - What content is considered most important? What topics or details are ignored?
   - What actions or work does the genre help make possible?
   - What actions or work does the genre make difficult?
   - What attitude toward readers is implied in the genre?
   - What attitude toward the world is implied in it?

7. Based on your analysis of the samples you've collected, *design or redesign a resource* for the Writing Center to teach writers and peer consultants about the genre.

8. *Schedule* a meeting with the Writing Center director or assistant director at least one week before your seminar presentation to debrief about your genre research, critique and revise the resource you've created, and plan your seminar activity.

9. *Share* what you've learned by leading us in a thirty-minute *activity* and *discussion* to help us learn about your chosen genre.

10. *Upload* your genre samples and resources to the seminar Webcourse.

Genres to Choose From

In the Writing Center, we often see assignments that don't seem to fit a recognizable genre. Such "mutt genres," as Elizabeth Wardle (2009) has termed them, are commonplace in school. For this assignment, we'll avoid these idiosyncratic occasions for writing and focus, instead, on the following commonplace genres used in multiple disciplines. The goal is to learn about genres you and the writers you work with are most likely to encounter in the university. Pick one to study:

- Abstract/summary
- Annotated bibliography
- Business letter
- Cover letter
- Critical review of a book, play, or film
- Lab/experimental research report (IMRaD format: Introduction, Method, Results, and Discussion)

- Library-based/secondary research report
- Literary analysis
- Literature review
- Personal statement/application essay
- Reaction paper
- Reflection
- Report of fieldwork/ethnographic research
- Research/grant proposal
- Resume/CV
- Thesis/dissertation
- Other commonplace genre

Further Recommended Reading

- Bawarshi, Anis, and Mary Jo Reiff. "Rhetorical Genre Studies." *Genre: An Introduction to History, Theory, Research, and Pedagogy.* Lafayette, IN: Parlor Press and The WAC Clearinghouse, 2010. 189–209.
- Carter, Michael. "Ways of Knowing, Doing, and Writing in the Disciplines." *College Composition and Communication* 58.3 (2007): 385–418.
- Carter, Michael, Carolyn R. Miller, and Ann M. Penrose. "Effective Composition Instruction: What Does the Research Show?" *Center for Communication in Science, Technology, and Management* 3 (April 1998): 1–11.
- Gordon, Layne M. P. "Beyond Generalist vs. Specialist: Making Connections Between Genre Theory and Writing Center Pedagogy. "*Praxis: A Writing Center Journal* 11.2 (2014): n.p. 20 Jul. 2014.
- Harrington, Anne, and Charles Moran, editors. *Genre Across the Curriculum.* Logan, UT: Utah State UP, 2005.
- Fitzgerald, Lauren, and Melissa Inanetta. "Tutoring Writing in and Across the Disciplines." *The Oxford Guide for Writing Tutors.* New York, NY: Oxford UP, 2015. 139–57.
- Johns, Ann M. "Genre Awareness for the Novice Academic Student." *Language Teaching* 41.2 (2008): 237–52.

* * *

As a result of this inquiry, tutors worked together to learn about several of the genres listed in the assignment above. They interviewed faculty and other professionals who use and teach the genres. They collected multiple and varied sample texts and studied them through the lens of genre analysis. They studied style guides, textbooks, and manuals intended to teach the genres. Again and again, collaborative inquiry groups came to more complex understandings, not only of specific genres but also of the concept of "genre" and just what a genre-based pedagogy for writing centers might entail. As a result, peer consultants questioned and revised a number of long-time handouts used in our writing center, which tutors came to see as oversimplified genres, promoting a fill-in-the-blank approach to genre as "form," rather than genre as social action. Tutors also designed new resources, both digital and print, some for tutors, others for writers. Two consultants established a wiki to share ideas and resources and to offer peer feedback on artifacts in process.

Katherine Gottschalk and Keith Hjortshoj (2004) distinguish between two conflicting models of education, one focused on *knowledge*, the other on *inquiry*. The first views "teaching as an opportunity to tell students what we know about a subject." The second views "teaching as an opportunity to engage students in the kinds of inquiry—and thus the kinds of thinking and learning—we pursue" (Gottschalk and Hjortshoj 2004, 21). While a *knowledge stance* supplies—and thereby limits—resources for learning, an *inquiry stance* expands resources for learning, based on the interests of writing consultants themselves. Fostering an inquiry stance toward writing center work, the "Problems of Practice Inquiry" is a powerful tool for the professional development of writing center consultants. It is a mechanism for building a community of practice and for expanding ways of thinking about and doing writing center work. Although the writing center is not studied systematically, it is, nevertheless, a research site, a starting point for inquiry, whose findings are related back to the center, prompting further research. As consultants pose questions, look critically at the work we do, talk to one another, and explore a variety of resources, they generate new knowledge. In this way, the "Problems of Practice Inquiry" is not intended to make writing consultants faithful implementers of received knowledge. Rather, it introduces consultants to received knowledge, via their own agendas. If it works well, this assignment encourages consultants to join in conversations about writing center research, theory, and practice, to debate the merits of received knowledge, and to test it against their own experiences in our local context. While the framing of inquiry described here relies heavily on secondary resources, others might adapt this model to act more as a catalyst for primary research, especially undergraduate research (Fitzgerald 2014). Readers might also imagine ways to use inquiry to foster new and innovative cross-institutional conversations and research among writing centers. Likewise, as Condon and Olson (2016) recommend, "our individual and collective praxis might be better shaped by sharing our culture of inquiry with the writers with whom we work" (34). Systematic, intentional study by tutors of their theories and practices, as well as the operations and conceptual frameworks that structure the writing centers in which they work, calls on us to imagine a writing center tutor inquiry movement oriented around these important questions:

- How might tutor inquiry benefit our writing centers and the staff who work in them?
- What various forms might tutor inquiry take—and with what consequences?
- What must writing center administrators do to structure and enable an inquiry stance toward writing center work?
- How might writing centers work collaboratively, both within and across institutions, to identify and study new contexts for tutor inquiry?

Notes

1. An abbreviated version of this chapter was previously published in *The Writing Lab Newsletter.* 37.5–6 (2013): 1–7.
2. Adapted from Harvey, Stephanie, and Harvey Daniels. *Comprehension & Collaboration: Inquiry Circles in Action.* Portsmouth, NH: Heinemann, 2009.

7

CONCLUSIONS

Research tells us that listening with empathy is the basis for a host of important workplace skills and strategies—assessing situations, making rational decisions, generating connections between theory and practice, arriving at deeper understandings about beliefs, adapting to new perspectives, informing instructional decisions, challenging traditions, improving teaching and learning, and validating ideals
— Mary Renck Jalongo (2008),
Learning to Listen, Listening to Learn

The five preceding chapters work together to make two arguments: first, writing center tutor education ought to be grounded in principles of inquiry-based teaching and learning. A central goal of tutor training ought to be to grow and develop in tutors the habits of mind that mark an inquiry-based approach to writing center work. Second, the everyday documents of writing center work—many of which, like those around which the previous chapters are organized, concern tutor education—ought to be carefully theorized. Doing so brings to the fore the principles and propositions that underpin writing center work, drawing attention to the ways that the theories that guide us operate together— and sometimes contradict—to ground our work. Too often, we create this or that mundane document without considering the conceptual frameworks upon which it is built. As a result, theory and practice may conflict. For example, a programmatic assessment report might detail numbers of students served, numbers of consultations, workshops, and so forth. But without an explicit theory of learning and a deliberate valuing of tutor education in particular, it might leave out this significant aspect of a writing center's work, neglecting that peer tutors, too, are learners whose professional development might also be measured and highlighted as a central mission of a writing center. But with explicit theorizing of writing center documents, we can bring theory and practice into alignment—or at least make the tensions between them conscious, productive. To return to Nordlof (2014) again, "the typical role of theory within a discipline is to provide a broad explanation of the processes

DOI: 10.7330/9781607325826.c007

that underlie the surface phenomenon that can be observed. In other words, theories provide the 'why' to help us understand the 'what'" (47). When theory and practice are brought to the fore in this way, then the question isn't what document to write, but what are my underlying values, assumptions, and beliefs, and how does this document enact, support, and advance them? How do we assess a document's practicality? In what ways do we evaluate its success or failure? To paraphrase Zebroski (1994) again, as soon as we pose these questions, we are always already involved in theorizing (15).

Theorizing writing center work is enabled by the principles of inquiry-based teaching and learning. Importantly, engaging tutors in this work is aimed not merely at individual change, but at creating a writing center as a *learning organization*. Alexandra Weinbaum et al. (2004) explain:

> Organizational theorists argue that there are two forms of learning in an organization: operational and conceptual. Operational learning has to do with technical know-how and procedures; conceptual learning involves thinking about why things are done and sometimes challenging the prevailing conditions; this involves identifying and articulating tacit images of how things work or how people characteristically behave. Once these have been acknowledged, it is possible to develop a new framework or mental model for an organization. Clearly both operational and conceptual learning are needed to make an organization functional; these two types of learning can be seen as paralleling the "facts/information" and "concepts" of individual learning. (23)

Because writing centers are typically inhabited by a constant influx of newcomers, both tutors and administrators, initiating and sustaining a writing center as a learning organization is a persistent challenge. Through an analysis of an assemblage of everyday writing center documents and the activities that circulate around them, this book argues for a variety of practices that work to build and maintain a writing center learning community, firmly grounded in research and theory. In order for a writing center to become a learning organization, administrators and tutors must engage together to examine unspoken assumptions, mental models, conceptual frameworks, to make them explicit in order to develop new, shared models.

In making a case for researching writing centers, Janice Neuleib and Maurice Sharton ask, "What happens when we look at ourselves through the eyes of the anthropologist and the archeologist?" (Neuleib and Scharton 1994, 57). Via the preceding chapters, I've argued that one way of "excavating our assumptions," as Neuleib and Sharton put it, is to study the everyday documents that structure writing center work. These documents tell us who we are, where we have been, and where we are going. They create and reflect the conceptual underpinnings, the values, assumptions, and beliefs—the habits of mind—that support our work, our decision-making, and our institutional and professional identities. To understand writing centers in the present, Neuleib and Sharton argue for a return to their beginnings. With this idea in mind, I'd like to return to the first focal document, the list of "20 Valued Practices for Tutoring Writing" in chapter 1. Further examination of the origins of this document draws attention to the fact that its beginning was *not* in a deliberate, carefully preconceived assessment plan or a novel approach to tutor education. Instead, the genesis for this document was failure. This origin story is the part I left out of the earlier chapter.

In my first semester directing the Writing Center at UCF, I moved too quickly to make big changes, with significant negative consequences. Among those changes, the workspace, I decided, needed a complete overhaul. Before my arrival, plans were already in motion to move the Writing Center from its long-time home in a "temporary" building, which had clearly seen better days, to a newly renovated space, currently under construction. This move couldn't come quickly enough as far as I was concerned. I was driven to distraction by the wasps swarming outside the front entrance and the ants crawling up my leg as I worked at my office desk. But long-time tutors seemed happy and comfortable in the familiar triple-wide trailer, even wistful about leaving it behind. They tutored unperturbed by the summer showers that routinely brought rain pouring in. Peer consultants simply moved a trashcan under the leak in the ceiling, covered the nearby computers with plastic trash bags, and kept right on working. Filled with funky old lamps, sprung couches, and discarded futons, its walls papered with clever posters designed by peer consultants to promote the Writing Center, and littered with a collection of tattered board games, this space had the look and feel of a dorm room or a basement playroom for boomerang children. Mindful of Jackie Grutsch McKinney's (2013) caution about conflicting values surrounding cultural notions of "homey" or "comfortable" writing center spaces, I prepared for the impending move across campus by dismantling the old home in favor of a new, modern, more professional workspace, one filled with sleek, contemporary office furniture and the latest technologies for digital composing (McKinney 2013, 20). I tossed out the posters and announced that we would not be using our weekly staff meetings to design new ones, as had been the recent custom. Instead, tutors would be assigned to read and discuss writing center research and theory and to develop inquiry questions to investigate.

At the same time, I initiated other changes to tutor education and professional development. In response, a handful of newcomers appeared indifferent, while a number of long-time consultants revolted. Some were quiet about it, merely avoiding me, sidestepping new requirements, while keeping up the appearance of cooperation. Others were more vocal, with a couple quitting the Writing Center altogether. With habits of mind attuned to an operational or instrumental approach to tutoring, consultants resisted the move to an inquiry-driven approach to writing center work, grounded in theory and research. For a time, I worked to convince them. But as tensions rose, I came to wonder if the problem was with me. Instead of rushing to change a well-established, successful writing center I knew little about, imposing my will on tutors I'd only just met, I needed to stop, step back, and take time to learn from them what they were doing, how, and why. I needed to learn their prior knowledge and current values. In short, I needed to listen more.

While listening is at the heart of writing center work, it is a subject writing center scholarship suggests we don't know much about. Rebecca Day Babcock et al. (2012), in their *A Synthesis of Qualitative Studies of Writing Center Tutoring, 1983–2006*, cite only four studies focused on listening (41–42). Likewise, listening researchers themselves are vocal about the gaps in knowledge in their field. Several lament the dearth of research concerning listening in interpersonal communication contexts—like writing centers. Graham Bodie (2011), for example, points out, "[T]here is not a single theory of interpersonal communication that directly addresses listening or places it as a central aspect of study. Instead, our field has assumed instead of problematized the concept of listening" (3). As in writing center studies, specialists in interpersonal communication have simply taken listening for granted. The study of listening is further vexed because experts don't agree on how to define listening. While specialists debate competing definitions of listening, a 2008 white paper, sponsored by the Research Committee of the International Listening Association (2008), recommends that the field let go of its insistence on a unified definition. Instead, the committee advocates theory-building, based on research from a variety of methodological perspectives. In short, listening researchers are coming to understand that listening is more complex than previously thought, and definitely not a set of skills to be taken for granted or considered obvious. My own failure to listen led me to consult listening research and to think more deliberately about the importance of listening in writing center contexts. Effective tutor education, I've learned, is an exercise in listening. Building and maintaining a writing center as a learning organization, grounded in research and theory, doesn't happen on command. It requires trust built over time, which depends on active, generous listening. At the same time, Babcock et al.'s (2012) survey of research on listening in writing centers reminds us that, as in the fields of listening and interpersonal communication, writing center studies, too, have significant gaps in our understanding of listening. We have a lot to learn about listening.

Listening to tutors in my own writing center—or failing to—and listening to one document's origin story brings to mind the wider conversation among writing center specialists concerning the stories of our work. In *Peripheral Visions for Writing Centers*, McKinney (2013) researches the stories we tell of our writing centers—at home behind closed doors, across our institutions, and, more broadly, as a discipline. What, she wonders, are the consequences of these stories? What work do they afford? What work do they inhibit? What do they help us to see and do? Whose interests do they serve? Equally important, in the telling and retelling some stories, what other stories don't get told—and with what consequences? McKinney argues that a grand narrative of writing center work occludes other "peripheral" stories. In this way, she questions deeply held assumptions about writing centers to prompt more varied, complex understandings of our work. While this grand narrative has served effectively to bind us together as a field of study and to communicate certain aspects of writing center work, McKinney argues that it also constrains us from seeing—and thus valuing and arguing for—other equally important aspects. In short, *Peripheral Visions* invites us to *see* writing center work differently, to bring into our field of vision those little narratives that have been overshadowed by the grand one.

In a similar spirit, I propose that, in addition to *seeing* differently, writing centers might also draw insights from research into listening to *listen* differently as well, to the documents of writing center work and to the complex of activities that circulate around them. I hope the document-based chapters of this book have demonstrated that through the everyday documents of writing center work we may find engaging new research questions and agendas. To more fully understand writing center work, we need to listen to not only individual documents and the activities they mediate but also to assemblages of documents. Collections of writing center documents can serve as focal points for listening to and excavating underlying values, assumptions, beliefs, and the habits of mind that guide what we do, how, and why. Together, they construct and reflect persistent themes and patterns.

Returning to Bruno Latour (2005), in *Reassembling the Social*, he asserts that the field of sociology rests on shaky ground, with the ambiguous term "the social" treated as a foundational given, upon which further knowledge is built. But, he challenges, what does "the social" mean, exactly? As a corrective, Latour proposes taking "the social" out of its black box to investigate just how it is constituted. He offers Actor-Network-Theory (ANT), situated within the sociology of science and technology, as a method for identifying the associations, including actors, agents, and activities that make up the social. Importantly, ANT asserts that non-humans also exert agency in our networks. Only by examining this "assemblage" of relations, argues Latour, can we posit a conceptual understanding of the social. Tracing mundane interactions between connected sites and actors allows us to see how they mediate between one another. Just as Latour proposes unpacking "the social" via examination of a constellation of constitutive relations, so we might better understand writing center work by asking, "Who interacts with what, and how? Of what associations, involving what actors, agents, and activities is a writing center made?" In this way, the five documents that animate this book are an assemblage. These documents, and others like them, are significant in their capacity as actants. Taking up Latour's idea of "tracing associations" among these assembled documents and the activities they generate shows how they become ways of rendering possibilities, communicating values and objectives, having conversations, engaging a culture of collaborative inquiry. In this way, everyday documents play an integral role in shaping and developing a writing center's actor-network.

Figure 7.1 illustrates some of the associations I've traced among the documents and related activities examined in each of the preceding chapters.

Starting with one document, just off center, the "20 Valued Practices for Tutoring Writing" from chapter 2, we can see that at least three other sets of documents and activities are associated with it, including program assessment, tutor education, and research. In addition, in the lower left-hand corner, this network also includes some of the texts/frameworks for analyzing this list of valued practices. The most crowded node is the one labeled "Tutor Education," to which each of the other focal documents featured in this book is linked. While there are many ways to trace associations, and multiple stories such a tracing might tell, by bringing together the assemblage that organizes this book, we can see the ways my work as a writing center administrator turns persistently to matters of tutor education. This document set tells that story. Together, this assemblage, always in motion and flux, reflects an emergent

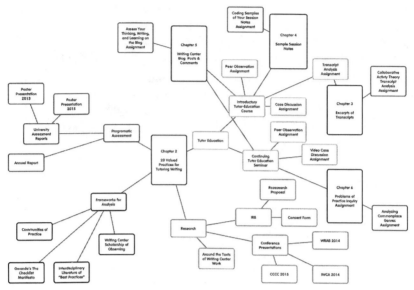

Figure 7.1. Writing Center Documents Network

professional identity, one based on the belief that while there are many important and pressing matters to juggle in writing center work, none is more important to me than effective tutor education and professional development. Over time, research such as that from the *Peer Writing Tutor Alumni Research Project* has confirmed my commitment that tutor education entails much more than merely "training" tutors to facilitate writing instruction. Rather, high-quality tutor education is grounded in research and theory, motivated by the principles of inquiry-based teaching and learning. As such, its reach extends far beyond the walls of the writing center. It can root tutors in habits of mind useful for a lifetime of meaningful work, communication, civic engagement, and relationships. Likewise, tutor education, in my experience, connects to every other aspect of writing center work. For example, the top left-hand corner shows a constellation of documents and activities related to program assessment, while the bottom right-hand corner includes a node that connects our "20 Valued Practices" to documents and activities related to scholarly research, including multiple conference presentations and this manuscript. "20 Valued Practices," as it turns out, mediates lots of different work in our writing center.

In addition to helping us to understand what we do, what we value, and who we are, listening to the everyday documents of writing center work may prompt new research agendas as well as new theoretical perspectives, which may then be tested, critiqued, amended, complicated, and extended. The end goal of an inquiry approach to writing center work and its constitutive documents need not be merely local knowledge, however. As Cochran-Smith and Lytle (2009) argue:

> Our perspective on local knowledge is somewhat different from some other descriptions of practitioner research, particularly action research . . . which explicitly state that the end goal is local action, not knowledge production. Our notion of local knowledge of practice challenges the view of knowledge production as something disembodied from the knower and the context and therefore untenable. We argue instead that the interpretive frameworks, conceptions, theories, and strategies generated by practitioner researchers in one local context are often pertinent to the work of . . . other local contexts. (95–96)

To make insights gained from inquiry into local writing center documents pertinent to the broader writing center community, I propose the following questions to ask about your own everyday documents:

- Why and how was the document created? By whom? To serve what ends? What was its exigency, its origin?
- What agendas inform the document?
- What work does the document do? What activities does it mediate, how, and why?
- How is the document understood and used by various stakeholders? In what ways does it circulate within and/or beyond the writing center?
- What values, assumptions, beliefs, habits of mind, and identities does the document create and reflect? How do these match up or conflict with guiding principles as reflected in other local documents and activities?
- What tools, such as activity theory, genre analysis, or discourse analysis, might be useful for explicating the document?
- In what ways does the document reflect, extend, complicate, or reject writing center values and practices expressed more broadly, beyond the specific, local context?
- If the document has been revised over time, if it has risen to prominence, or fallen away, what is the significance of these changes?
- What do we hear when we listen, really listen, to the documents and the accompanying activities that structure our work? What do collections or assemblages of documents reveal, together, about our principles and commitments? How do they define the nature of writing center work?

REFERENCES

Ambrose, Susan A., Michael W. Bridges, Michele DiPietro, Marsh C. Lovett, and Marie K. Norman. 2010. *How Learning Works: Seven Research-Based Principles for Smart Teaching.* San Francisco: Jossey-Bass.

Archer, Maureen Morrissey. 1996. "Assessing Tutorials from the Inside: Interactive Exams." *Writing Lab Newsletter* 21 (2): 4–7.

Argyris, Chris. 1991. "Teaching Smart People How to Learn." *Harvard Business Review* 69 (3): 4–15.

Babcock, Rebecca Day, Kellye Manning, Travis Rogers, Courtney Goff, and Amanda McCain. 2012. *A Synthesis of Qualitative Studies of Writing Center Tutoring, 1983–2006.* New York: Peter Lang.

Babcock, Rebecca Day, and Terese Thonus. 2012. *Researching the Writing Center: Towards an Evidence-Based Practice.* New York: Peter Lang. http://dx.doi.org/10.3726/978-1-4539-08 69-3.

Baer, Melinda. 2006. "Using Weblogs in Your Writing Center." *Writing Lab Newsletter* 31 (2): 1–4.

Bawarshi, Anis, and Mary Jo Reiff. 2010. *Genre: An Introduction to History, Theory, Research, and Pedagogy.* Lafayette, IN: Parlor Press and The WAC Clearinghouse.

Beck, Isabel L., Margaret G. McKeown, Cheryl Sandora, Linda Kucan, and Jo Worthy. 1996. "Questioning the Author: A Yearlong Classroom Implementation to Engage Students with Text." *Elementary School Journal* 96 (4): 385–414. http://dx.doi.org/10 .1086/461835.

Bell, James C. 2001. "Tutor Training and Reflection on Practice." *Writing Center Journal* 21 (2): 79–98.

Berry, Landon, and Brandy Dieterle. 2016. "Group Consultations: Developing Dedicated, Technological Spaces for Collaborative Writing and Learning." *Computers and Composition* 41: 18–31. http://www.sciencedirect.com/science/article/pii/S8755461516300044.

Bird, Barbara. 2012. "Rethinking our View of Learning." *Writing Lab Newsletter* 36 (5–6): 1–5.

Birks, Melanie, and Jane Mills. 2015. *Grounded Theory: A Practical Guide.* 2nd ed. Los Angeles: Sage.

Black, Laurel. 1998. *Between Talk and Teaching: Reconsidering the Writing Conference.* Logan: Utah State University Press.

Bodie, Graham. 2011. "The Understudied Nature of Listening in Interpersonal Communication: Introduction to a Special Issue." *International Journal of Listening* 25 (1–2): 1–9. http://dx.doi.org/10.1080/10904018.2011.536462.

Bowden, Darsie. 1995. "Inter-Activism: Strengthening the Writing Conference." *Writing Center Journal* 15 (2): 163–80.

Broglie, Mary. 1990. "From Teacher to Tutor: Making the Change." *Writing Lab Newsletter* 15 (4): 1–3.

Cain, Kathleen Shine. 2010. To WCenter discussion list, October 2.

"Call for Submissions." 2010. *Writing Center Journal* 31 (1): 116.

Camp, Heather. 2007. "Context Matters: Incorporating Tutor Development into the Writing Center." *Writing Lab Newsletter* 31 (9): 1–5.

Cardaro, Danielle. 2014. "Practical Uses for Session Reports Among Faculty: A Case Study." *Writing Lab Newsletter* 38 (9–10): 1–6.

DOI: 10.7330/9781607325826.c008

Carter, Michael, Carolyn R. Miller, and Ann M. Penrose. 1998. "Effective Composition Instruction: What Does the Research Show?" *Center for Communication in Science, Technology, and Management* 3 (April): 1–11.

Charmaz, Kathy. 2014. *Constructing Grounded Theory*. 2nd ed. Los Angeles: Sage.

Christensen, Peter Holdt. 2007. "Knowledge Sharing: Moving Away from the Obsession with Best Practices." *Journal of Knowledge Management* 11 (1): 36–47. http://dx.doi.org /10.1108/13673270710728222.

Clark, Irene. 1999. "Addressing Genre in the Writing Center." *Writing Center Journal* 20 (1): 7–32.

Cochran-Smith, Marilyn, and Susan L. Lytle. 2009. *Inquiry as Stance: Practitioner Research for the Next Generation*. New York: Teachers College Press.

Coffield, Frank, and Shelia Edward. 2009. "Rolling Out 'Good,' 'Best,' and 'Excellent' Practice. What's Next? Perfect Practice?" *British Educational Research Journal* 35 (3): 371–90. http://dx.doi.org/10.1080/01411920802044396.

Cogie, Jane. 1998. "In Defense of Conference Summaries: Widening the Reach of Writing Center Work." *Writing Center Journal* 18 (2): 47–70.

Condon, Frankie, and Bobbi Olson. 2016. "Building a House for Linguistic Diversity: Writing Centers, English-Language Teaching and Learning, and Social Justice." In *Tutoring Second Language Writers*, ed. Shanti Bruce and Ben Rafoth, 27–52. Logan: Utah State University Press.

Conway, Glenda. 1998. "Reporting Writing Center Sessions to Faculty: Pedagogical and Ethical Concerns." *Writing Lab Newsletter* 22 (8): 9–12.

Crockett, Michele D. 2002. "Inquiry as Professional Development: Creating Dilemmas through Teachers' Work." *Teaching and Teacher Education* 18 (5): 609–24. http://dx.doi.org /10.1016/S0742-051X(02)00019-7.

Devet, Bonnie. 1990. "A Method for Observing and Evaluating Writing Lab Tutorials." *Writing Center Journal* 10 (2): 65–83.

Dias, Patrick, Aviva Freedman, Peter Medway, and Anthony Paré. 1999. *Worlds Apart: Acting and Writing in Academic and Workplace Contexts*. Mahwah, NJ: Lawrence Erlbaum.

Dinitz, Sue, and Susanmarie Harrington. 2014. "The Role of Disciplinary Expertise in Shaping Writing Tutorials." *Writing Center Journal* 33 (2): 73–98.

Donaldson, Stewart I., Laura E. Gooler, and Michael Scriven. 2002. "Strategies for Managing Evaluation Anxiety: Toward a Psychology of Program Evaluation." *American Journal of Evaluation* 23 (3): 261–73. http://dx.doi.org/10.1177/109821400202300303.

Driscoll, Dana Lynn, and Sherry Wynn Perdue. 2012. "Theory, Lore, and More: An Analysis of RAD Research in The Writing Center Journal, 1980–2009." *Writing Center Journal* 32 (2): 11–39.

Driscoll, Dana Lynn, and Sherry Wynn Perdue. 2014. "RAD Research as a Framework for Writing Center Inquiry: Survey and Interview Data on Writing Center Administrators' Beliefs about Research and Research Practices." *Writing Center Journal* 34 (1): 105–33.

Engeström, Yrjö, and Reijo Miettinen. 1999. "Introduction." In *Perspectives on Activity Theory*, ed. Yrjö Engestrom, Reijo Miettinen, and Raija-Leena Punamaki, 1–16. Cambridge: Cambridge University Press. http://dx.doi.org/10.1017/CBO9780511812 774.002.

Feek, Warren. 2007. "Best of Practices?" *Development in Practice* 17 (4–5): 653–55. http://dx .doi.org/10.1080/09614520701469898.

Fels, Dawn. 2010. To WCenter discussion list, August 29.

Fisher, Douglas, and Nancy Frey. 2004. *Improving Adolescent Literacy: Strategies That Work*. Upper Saddle River, NJ: Pearson.

Fitzgerald, Lauren. 2014. "Undergraduate Writing Tutors as Researchers: Redrawing Boundaries." *Writing Center Journal* 33 (2): 17–35.

Fitzgerald, Lauren, and Melissa Ianetta. 2015. *The Oxford Guide for Writing Tutors*. New York: Oxford University Press.

Freedman, Aviva. 1995. "The What, When, Where, Why, and How of Classroom Genres." In *Reconceiving Writing, Rethinking Writing Instruction*, ed. Joseph Petraglia, 121–44. Mahwah, NJ: Lawrence Erlbaum.

Gardner, Clint. 2008. "Writing Center Blogs." *PeerCentered* (blog), March 25.

Gawande, Atul. 2009. *The Checklist Manifesto: How to Get Things Right.* New York: Picador.

Gee, James Paul. 2005. *An Introduction to Discourse Analysis: Theory and Method.* 2nd ed. New York: Routledge.

Gee, James Paul. 2013. *The Anti-Education Era: Creating Smarter Students through Digital Learning.* New York: Palgrave.

Gee, James Paul. 2014. *How to Do Discourse Analysis: A Toolkit.* 2nd ed. New York: Routledge.

Geller, Anne Ellen, and Harry Denny. 2013. "Of Lady Bugs, Low Status, and Loving the Job: Writing Center Professionals Navigating Their Careers." *Writing Center Journal* 33 (1): 96–129.

Geller, Anne Ellen, Michele Eodice, Frankie Condon, Meg Carroll, and Elizabeth Boquet. 2007. *The Everyday Writing Center: A Community of Practice.* Logan: Utah State University Press.

Gilewicz, Magdalena, and Terese Thonus. 2003. "Close Vertical Transcription in Writing Center Training and Research." *Writing Center Journal* 24 (1): 25–49.

Gillam, Alice. 2002. "The Call to Research: Early Representations of Writing Center Research." In *Writing Center Research: Extending the Conversation*, ed. Paula Gillespie, Alice Gillam, Lady Falls Brown, and Byron Stay, 3–23. Mahwah, NJ: Erlbaum.

Gillespie, Paula. 2002. "Beyond the House of Lore: WCenter as Research Site." In *Writing Center Research: Extending the Conversation*, ed. Paula Gillespie, Alice Gillam, Lady Falls Brown, and Byron Stay, 39–51. Mahwah, NJ: Erlbaum.

Gillespie, Paula, and Neal Lerner. 2008. *The Longman Guide to Peer Tutoring.* 2nd ed. New York: Pearson/Longman.

Gottschalk, Katherine, and Keith Hjortshoj. 2004. *The Elements of Teaching Writing: A Resource for Instructors in All Disciplines.* Boston, MA: Bedford.

Graziano-King, Janine, and Hope Parisi. 2011. "Integrating Best Practices: Learning Communities and the Writing Center." *Community College Enterprise* 17 (1): 23–39.

Greiner, Alexis. 2000 "Tutoring in Unfamiliar Subjects." In *A Tutor's Guide Helping Writers One to One*, ed. Ben Rafoth, 85–90. Portsmouth, NH: Heinemann.

Griggs, Claudine. 2012. "Director as Client: Participatory Observations in the Writing Center." *Writing Lab Newsletter* 36 (9–10): 6–10.

Grimm, Nancy. 1999. *Good Intentions: Writing Center Work for Postmodern Times.* Portsmouth, NH: Heinemann.

Grimm, Nancy. 2003. "In the Spirit of Service: Making Writing Center Research a 'Featured Character'." In *The Center Will Hold: Critical Perspectives on Writing Center Scholarship*, ed. Michael A. Pemberton and Joyce Kinkead, 41–57. Logan: Utah State University Press.

Grimm, Nancy. 2009. "New Conceptual Frameworks for Writing Center Work." *Writing Center Journal* 29 (2): 11–27.

Griswold, W. Gary. 2006. "Postsecondary Reading: What Writing Center Tutors Need to Know." *Journal of College Reading and Learning* 37 (1): 59–72. http://dx.doi.org/10.1080/10790195.2006.10850193.

Hall, R. Mark. 2011. "Using Dialogic Reflection to Develop a Writing Center Community of Practice." *Writing Center Journal* 31 (1): 82–105.

Hall, R. Mark. 2013. "Problems of Practice: An Inquiry Stance toward Writing Center Work." *Writing Lab Newsletter* 37 (5–6): 1–7.

Hardman, Joanne, and Alan Amory. 2015. "Introduction to Cultural-Historical Activity Theory and Tool Mediation." In *Activity Theory, Authentic Learning and Emerging Technologies*, ed. Vivienne Bozalek, Dick Ng'ambi, Denise Wood, Jan Herrington, Joanne Hardman, and Alan Amory, 9–21. London: Routledge.

Harris, Jeanette, Leonard A. Podis, JoAnne M. Podis, Ben Rafoth, James A. Inman, Donna N. Sewell, Robert W. Barnett, Jacob S. Blumner, and Nancy Maloney Grimm. 2001. "Review: Reaffirming, Reflecting, Reforming: Writing Center Scholarship Comes of Age." *College English* 63 (5): 662–8. http://dx.doi.org/10.2307/379050.

Harris, Muriel. 2001. "Collaboration Is Not Collaboration Is Not Collaboration: Writing Center Tutorials vs. Peer-Response Groups." In *The Allyn and Bacon Guide to Writing Center Theory and Practice*, ed. Robert W. Barnett and Jacob S. Blumner, 272–85. Boston: Allyn Bacon.

Harris, Muriel. 2006. "Using Tutorial Principles to Train Tutors: Practicing Our Praxis." In *The Writing Center Director's Resource Book*, ed. Christina Murphy and Byron L. Stay, 301–10. Mahwah, NJ: Lawrence Erlbaum.

Harris, Muriel, and Tony Silva. 1993. "Tutoring ESL Students: Issues and Options." *College Composition and Communication* 44 (4): 525–37. http://dx.doi.org/10.2307/358388.

Harvey, Stephanie, and Harvey Daniels. 2009. *Comprehension and Collaboration: Inquiry Circles in Action*. Portsmouth, NH: Heinemann.

Hewett, Beth. 2010. *The Online Writing Conference: A Guide for Teachers and Tutors*. Portsmouth, NH: Heinemann-Boynton/Cook.

Hillocks, George. 1995. *Teaching Writing as Reflective Practice*. New York: Teachers College Press.

Hsu, Pei-Ling. and Wolff-Michael Roth. 2008. "Lab Technicians and High School Student Interns—Who Is Scaffolding Whom?: On Forms of Emergent Expertise." *Science Education* 93 (1): 1–25. http://dx.doi.org/10.1002/sce.20289.

Hughes, Brad, Paula Gillespie, and Harvey Kail. 2010. "What They Take with Them: Findings from the Peer Writing Tutor Alumni Research Project." *Writing Center Journal* 30 (2): 12–46.

Ianetta, Melissa. 2015. "Tutor-Researchers in the Writing Center." Presentation at the International Writing Centers Association Conference, Pittsburgh, PA, October 8–10.

Irvine, Colin. 2012. "Taking on 'Best Practices': A Novel Response to Managerialism in Higher Education." *Pedagogy* 12 (3): 389–404. http://dx.doi.org/10.1215/15314200-16 25226.

Jackson, Kim. 1996. "Beyond Record-keeping: Session Reports and Tutor Education." *Writing Lab Newsletter* 20 (6): 11–3.

Jalongo, Mary Renck. 2008. *Learning to Listen, Listening to Learn: Building Essential Skills in Young Children*. Washington, DC: National Association for the Education of Young Children.

Jonassen, David H., and Lucia Rohrer-Murphy. 1999. "Activity Theory as a Framework for Designing Constructivist Learning Environments." *Educational Technology Research and Development* 47 (1): 61–79. http://dx.doi.org/10.1007/BF02299477.

Kanigel, Robert. 1997. "Taylor-Made (19th-Century Efficiency Expert Frederick Taylor)." *Sciences* 37 (3): 18–22. http://dx.doi.org/10.1002/j.2326-1951.1997.tb03309.x.

Kiedaisch, Jean, and Sue Dinitz. 2001. "Look Back and Say 'So What': The Limitations of the Generalist Tutor." In *The Allyn and Bacon Guide to Writing Center Theory and Practice*, ed. Robert W. Barnett and Jacob S. Blumner, 260–71. Boston: Allyn and Bacon.

Komara, Kirsten. 2006. "Mock Tutorials: A Dramatic Method for Training Tutors." *Writing Lab Newsletter* 30 (9): 12–5.

Lambert, Megan. 2015. "Understanding the Roles of Resources in Writing Center Tutoring Sessions." Master's thesis, University of Central Florida, Orlando.

Larrance, Anneke J., and Barbara Brady. 1995. "A Pictogram of Writing Center Conference Follow-up." *Writing Lab Newsletter* 20 (4): 5–7.

Latour, Bruno. 1987. *Science in Action*. Cambridge, MA: Harvard University Press.

Latour, Bruno. 2005. *Reassembling the Social: An Introduction to Actor-Network-Theory*. Oxford: Oxford University Press.

Lave, Jean, and Etienne Wenger. 1991. *Situated Learning: Legitimate Peripheral Participation.* Cambridge: Cambridge University Press. http://dx.doi.org/10.1017/CBO9780511815355.

Lavoie, Richard. 1989. *How Difficult Can This Be? The F.A.T. City Workshop—Understanding Learning Disabilities.* Films Media Group. Films on Demand. https://www.youtube.com/watch?v=0hUIXoV2rZc.

Law, Joe, and Christina Murphy. 1997. "Formative Assessment and the Paradigms of Writing Center Practice." *Clearing House: A Journal of Educational Strategies, Issues and Ideas* 71 (2): 106–108. http://dx.doi.org/10.1080/00098659709599336.

Lerner, Neal. 2007. "Situated Learning in the Writing Center." In *Marginal Word, Marginal Work? Tutoring the Academy in the Work of Writing Centers,* ed. William J. Macauley and Nicholas Mauriello, 53–73. Creskill, NJ: Hampton.

Lerner, Neal. 2014. "The Unpromising Present of Writing Center Studies: Author and Citation Patterns in *The Writing Center Journal,* 1980–2009." *Writing Center Journal* 34 (1): 67–102.

Lunsford, Andrea. 2003. "Collaboration, Control, and the Idea of a Writing Center." In *The St. Martin's Sourcebook for Writing Tutors,* 2nd ed., ed. Christina Murphy and Steve Sherwood, 46–53. Boston: Bedford/St. Martin's.

Malenczyk, Rita. 2013. "'I Thought I Put That in to Amuse You': Tutor Reports as Organizational Narrative." *Writing Center Journal* 33 (1): 74–95.

Mattison, Michael. 2007. "Someone to Watch Over Me: Reflection and Authority in the Writing Center." *Writing Center Journal* 27 (1): 29–51.

McCann, Thomas. 2014. *Transforming Talk into Text: Argument Writing, Inquiry, and Discussion, Grades 6–12.* New York: Teachers College Press.

McKinney, Jackie Grutsch. 2009. "Geek in the Center: Blogging." *Writing Lab Newsletter* 34 (1): 7–9.

McKinney, Jackie Grutsch. 2013. *Peripheral Visions for Writing Centers.* Logan: Utah State University Press.

McKinney, Jackie Grutsch. 2016. *Strategies for Writing Center Research.* Anderson, SC: Parlor Press.

Moberg, Eric. 2010. *The College Writing Center: Best Practices, Best Technologies. Report No. ED 508644.* ERIC Document; Retrieved May 28, 2013.

Moje, Elizabeth Birr, Allan Luke, Bronwyn Davies, and Brian Street. 2009. "Literacy and Identity: Examining the Metaphors in History and Contemporary Research." *Reading Research Quarterly* 44 (4): 415–37. http://dx.doi.org/10.1598/RRQ.44.4.7.

Munger, Roger H., Ilene Rubenstein, and Edna Burrow. 1996. "Observation, Interaction, and Reflection: The Foundation for Tutor Training." *Writing Lab Newsletter* 21 (4): 1–5.

Neff, Julie. 1994. "Learning Disabilities and the Writing Center." In *Intersections: Theory-Practice in the Writing Center,* ed. Joan A. Mullin and Ray Wallace, 81–95. Urbana, IL: NCTE.

Neuleib, Janice Witherspoon, and Maurice A. Scharton. 1994. "Writing Others, Writing Ourselves: Ethnography and the Writing Center." In *Intersections: Theory-Practice in the Writing Center,* ed. Joan Mullin and Ray Wallace, 54–67. Urbana: NCTE.

Nordlof, John. 2014. "Vygotsky, Scaffolding, and the Role of Theory in Writing Center Work." *Writing Center Journal* 34 (1): 45–64.

North, Stephen M. 1987. *The Making of Knowledge in Composition: Portrait of an Emerging Field.* Upper Montclair, NJ: Boynton/Cook.

Okawa, Gail Y., Thomas Fox, Lucy J.Y. Chang, Shana R. Windsor, Frank Bella Chavez, Jr., and Hayes LaGuan. 1991. "Multicultural Voices: Peer Tutoring and Critical Reflection in the Writing Center." *Writing Center Journal* 12 (1): 11–33.

Osburn, Joe, Guy Caruso, and Wolf Wolfensberger. 2011. "The Concept of 'Best Practice': A Brief Overview of Its Meanings, Scope, Uses, and Shortcomings." *International Journal*

of Disability Development and Education 58 (3): 213–22. http://dx.doi.org/10.1080/10349
12X.2011.598387.

Pemberton, Michael, and Joyce Kinkead, eds. 2003. *The Center Will Hold: Critical Perspectives
on Writing Center Scholarship.* Logan: Utah State University Press.

Pemberton, Michael A. 1995. "Writing Center Ethics: Sharers and Seclusionists." *Writing
Lab Newsletter* 20 (3): 13–4.

Petr, Christopher G., and Uta M. Walter. 2005. "Best Practices Inquiry: A Mulitdimentional,
Value-Critical Framework." *Journal of Social Work Education* 41 (2): 251–67. http://dx
.doi.org/10.5175/JSWE.2005.200303109.

Petraglia, Joseph. 1995. "Spinning Like a Kite: A Closer Look at the Pseudotransactional
Function of Writing." *Journal of Advanced Composition* 15 (1): 19–33.

Research Committee of the International Listening Association. 2008. *Priorities of
Listening Research: Four Interrelated Initiatives.* Belle Plaine, MN: International Listening
Association.

Rosner, Mary, and Megan Wann. 2010. "Talking Heads and Other Body Parts." *Writing Lab
Newsletter* 34 (6): 7–11.

Russell, David. 1995. "Activity Theory and Its Implications for Writing Instruction." In
Reconceiving Writing, Rethinking Writing Instruction, ed. Joseph Petraglia, 51–77. Mahwah,
NJ: Lawrence Erlbaum.

Schendel, Ellen, and William J. Macauley Jr. 2012. *Building Writing Center Assessments that
Matter.* Logan: Utah State University Press.

Sheridan, David, and James A. Inman, eds. 2010. *Multiliteracy Centers: Writing Center Work,
New Media, and Multimodal Rhetoric.* Creskill, NJ: Hampton.

Sherven, Keva N. 2010. "Worlds Collide: Integrating Writing Center Best Practices into
a First Year Composition Program." Master's thesis, Indiana University – Purdue
University Indianapolis.

Silk, Bobbie Bayliss, ed. 2002. *The Writing Center Resource Manual.* 2nd ed. Emmitsburg,
MD: NWCA Press.

Smith, Colleen, and Frances Sutton. 1999. "Best Practice: What It Is and What It Is Not."
International Journal of Nursing Practice 5 (2): 100–5. http://dx.doi.org/10.1046/j.1440-172
x.1999.00154.x.

Smith, Jane Bowman. 2005. "Tutor Training as Reflective Practice: Problem Setting and
Solving." *Writing Lab Newsletter* 29 (8): 13+.

Smith, John P., III, Andrea A. diSessa, and Jeremy Roschelle. 1993–1994. "Misconceptions
Reconceived: A Constructivist Analysis of Knowledge in Transition." *Journal of the
Learning Sciences* 3 (2): 115–63. http://dx.doi.org/10.1207/s15327809jls0302_1.

Spinuzzi, Clay. 2008. *Network: Theorizing Knowledge Work in Telecommunications.* Cambridge:
Cambridge University Press. http://dx.doi.org/10.1017/CBO9780511509605.

Stenberg, Shari J., and Darby Arant Whealy. 2009. "Chaos Is the Poetry: From Outcomes
to Inquiry in Service-Learning Pedagogy." *College Composition and Communication* 60
(4): 683–706.

Tamor, Lynne, and James T. Bond. 1983. "Text Analysis: Inferring Process from Product."
In *Research on Writing: Principles and Methods,* ed. Peter Mosenthal, Lynne Tamor, and
Sean A. Walmsley, 99–138. New York: Longman.

Thompson, Isabelle, and Jo Mackiewicz. 2014. *Talk about Writing: The Tutoring Strategies of
Experienced Writing Center Tutors.* New York: Routledge.

Thompson, Isabelle, Alyson Whyte, David Shannon, Amanda Muse, Kristen Miller, Milla
Chapell, and Abby Whigham. 2009. "Examining Our Lore: A Survey of Students' and
Tutors' Satisfaction with Writing Center Conferences." *Writing Center Journal* 29 (1):
78–105.

Thonus, Terese. 2014. "Tutoring Multilingual Students: Shattering the Myths." *Journal of College
Reading and Learning* 44 (2): 200–213. http://www.tandfonline.com/doi/abs/10.10
80/10790195.2014.906233.

Tierney, Robert J., and P. David Pearson. 1993. "Toward a Composing Model of Reading." *Language Arts* 60:568–80.

Toulmin, Stephen. 1999. "Knowledge as Shared Procedures." In *Perspectives on Activity Theory*, ed. Yrjö Engeström, Reijo Miettinen, and Raija-Leena Punamaki, 53–64. Cambridge: Cambridge University Press. http://dx.doi.org/10.1017/CBO9780511812774.005.

Trahan, Heather. 2012. "Queers, Cupid's Arrow, and Contradictions in the Classroom: An Activity Theory Analysis." *Journal of the Assembly for Expanded Perspectives on Learning* 18 (1): 56–69.

Van Slembrouck, Jane. 2010. "Watch and Learn: Peer Evaluation and Tutoring Pedagogy." *Praxis: A Writing Center Journal* 8 (1): n.p.

Vygotsky, Lev S. 1978. *Mind in Society: The Development of Higher Psychological Processes.* Ed. Michael Cole, Silvia Scribner Vera John-Steiner, and Ellen Souberman. Cambridge, MA: Harvard University Press.

Walker, Kristin. 1998. "The Debate Over Generalist and Specialist Tutors: Genre Theory's Contribution." *Writing Center Journal* 18 (2): 27–46.

Wardle, Elizabeth. 2009. "'Mutt Genres' and the Goal of FYC: Can We Help Students Write the Genres of the University?" *College Composition and Communication* 60 (4): 765–89.

Wardle, Elizabeth, and Doug Downs, eds. 2014. *Writing about Writing: A College Reader.* 2nd ed. Boston: Bedford/St. Martin's.

Weaver, Margaret. 2001. "Resistance Is Anything but Futile: Some More Thoughts on Writing Conference Summaries." *Writing Center Journal* 21 (2): 15–56.

Weinbaum, Alexandra, David Allen, and Tina Blythe. 2004. *Teaching as Inquiry: Asking Hard Questions to Improve Practice and Student Achievement.* New York: Teachers College Press.

Wells, Gordon. 2000. "Dialogic Inquiry in Education: Building on the Legacy of Vygotsky." In *Vygotskian Perspectives on Literacy Research: Constructing Meaning through Collaborative Inquiry*, ed. Carol D. Lee and Peter Smagorinsky, 51–85. New York: Cambridge University Press.

Wenger, Etienne. 1998. *Communities of Practice: Learning, Meaning, and Identity.* Cambridge: Cambridge University Press. http://dx.doi.org/10.1017/CBO9780511803932.

Wenger, Etienne. 2006. *Communities of Practice: A Brief Introduction.*

Whitin, Phillis. 2007. "The Ties that Bind: Emergent Literacy and Scientific Inquiry." *Language Arts* 85 (1): 20–30.

Yancey, Kathleen Blake. 2002. "Seeing Practice through Their Eyes." In *Writing Center Research: Extending the Conversation*, ed. Paula Gillespie, Alice Gillam, Lady Falls Brown, and Byron Stay, 189–202. Mahwah, NJ: Erlbaum.

Zebroski, James Thomas. 1994. *Thinking through Theory: Vygotskian Perspectives on the Teaching of Writing.* Portsmouth, NH: Boynton/Cook.

ABOUT THE AUTHOR

R. MARK HALL is associate professor of rhetoric, composition, and literacy studies at the University of Central Florida, where he directs the University Writing Center. He has also led writing centers at California State University, Chico and the University of North Carolina at Charlotte. He has published chapters in several edited collections and articles in *College English*, *The Writing Center Journal*, *Writing Lab Newsletter*, *The Writing Instructor*, and *Praxis*.

INDEX